THE
NATIONAL
AIR
AND SPACE
MUSEUM

Acknowledgments

My participation in this volume grew out of an idle dinner conversation in Chicago with Ian Ballantine who, by casually mentioning old airplanes, inadvertently touched upon a childhood fascination with all things that flew that has continued in me up to the present. Our talk inevitably turned from there to one of my favorite places, the Smithsonian Institution, for I had been a steady visitor to the old Air Museum ever since it had opened in a Quonset off to one side of the "Castle." Moreover, my interest was clearly shared by more than twenty million people who had visited the new National Air and Space Museum in its first two years. When Ian mentioned that Harry N. Abrams, Inc., had an agreement with the Smithsonian Institution for publishing an authorized book on their new Museum, I immediately volunteered to write the text. Ever since that evening I have been assisted, educated, instructed, amused, and indulged by highly specialized men and women of the National Air and Space Museum staff whose knowledge and expertise are but imperfectly reflected by my text.

I could not have undertaken this work without the assistance and encouragement of Ian Ballantine and Harry N. Abrams, Inc.'s President Andrew Stewart and Digby Diehl, his editor-in-chief; nor would the work have progressed so pleasurably and smoothly without the extraordinarily able and professional Abrams' staff—in particular editor Edith Pavese and designer Nai Chang; but the book was made possible only by the complete and eager cooperation we all received from the staff of the National Air and Space Museum. In behalf of us all I would like to single out certain individuals whose unstinting giving of their time and expertise are owed recognition in print.

Michael Collins, Under Secretary of the Smithsonian Institution, and Melvin B. Zisfein, Deputy Director of NASM, lent their authority and approval to this project and made it possible for me to work from the Museum galleries' concept scripts. This pattern of management support continues under the new Director, Dr. Noel W. Hinners. Executive Officer Walter J. Boyne personally guided me through the Silver Hill Museum complex and the *Enola Gay*'s bomb bay, and subsequently guided the text through its rockier channels. Public Information Officer Lynne Murphy, her successor Rita Bobowski, and Staff Assistant Louise Hull provided invaluable contacts and administrative assistance.

It is said that a museum is only as good as its collection; but a collection is only as good as its curators. Paul Garber, NASM's Historian Emeritus, was responsible for many of the Museum's earliest acquisitions. Charles H. Gibbs-Smith, NASM's first Lindbergh Professor of Aerospace History, was extremely helpful with information on the Wrights. In the Aeronautics section, however, our gratitude is owed Assistant Director of Aeronautics Donald S. Lopez; Curator of Aircraft Louis S. Casey; Curator of Propulsion Robert B. Meyer; and Curators Robert C. Mikesh and Edmund T. Wooldridge. A very special thanks to Assistant Curator Claudia M. Oakes whose uncluttered writing and thinking, encouragement, knowledge, and humor made things far easier than they would otherwise have been. Thanks, too, to Museum Technician Jay P. Spenser and Museum Specialist Supervisor Elmont J. Thomas of the Aeronautics section.

Frederick C. Durant III, Assistant Director of Astronautics, was embarrassingly patient in answering my questions about spacecraft principles and generous in sharing his knowledge and appreciation of space pioneer Robert H. Goddard. If the space sections of this text appear at all learned they reflect the invaluable assistance and expertise of Walter H. Flint and Tom D. Crouch, Curators of Astronautics, and Gregory P. Kennedy and Walter J. Dillon, Assistant Curators.

Curator of Art James Dean was gracious enough to permit some of his art treasures to be sprinkled throughout this book despite the fact that the Art Gallery displays the collection more as a unified whole. And we thank, too, Bill Good and Mary Henderson of the Art Department for so generously giving their time.

I would like to acknowledge a special "writer's debt" to the Museum's Reference Librarian Dominick A. Pisano who tracked down some wonderful stories and leads, and Karl P. Suthard, a Technical Information Specialist in the Library. And for his help at the Silver Hill Museum, our gratitude to Edward Chalkley, that Museum complex's Assistant Chief.

Hernan Otano, Chief of the Audiovisual Unit, Richard Wakefield, A/V Supervisor, Electronic Technicians John Hartman and Daniel Philips, Exhibit Section's Chief of the Production Unit Frank Nelms, Exhibit Specialist Sylvandous Anderson, Painter Daniel Fletcher and Carpenter Milan Tomasevich all generously shared their materials, equipment, experience, and time.

Howard Wolko, Assistant Director of the Science and Technology section, and Curators Richard Hallion and Paul Hanle helped me feel almost comfortable in writing about what had previously been incomprehensible. I am grateful, too, to Robert W. Wolfe, a geologist with the Center for Earth and Planetary Studies, for his assistance and Von Del Chamberlain, Chief of the Presentations Division, and Patricia Woodside for their help on the Albert Einstein Spacearium section.

Joseph Davisson, NASM's Building Manager, Claude Russell, Assistant Building Manager, Supervisor Mary Whittaker, and Artifacts Crewman Larry Johnson helped make the inaccessible accessible. Captain Preston Herald III, Captain of the Museum's Protection Division, and his staff saw that we were able to freely wander about.

And finally, I would like to acknowledge my genuine debt to a great many writers who have so generously permitted me to quote from their articles and books.

C.D.B. Bryan
Guilford, Conn.

THE NATIONAL AIR AND SPACE MUSEUM

Volume One
AIR

Text by **C.D.B. BRYAN**

Art Direction & Design by **DAVID LARKIN**

PEACOCK PRESS/BANTAM BOOKS
Toronto   New York   London   Sydney

to my great-great uncle

CAPT. JOHN RANDOLPH BRYAN, C.S.A.

who, as aide-de-camp to General J. B. Magruder, made three balloon ascensions for the Army of the Peninsula, the last of which, on May 5, 1862, became an inadvertent free flight because a young soldier became entangled in the guide-rope connecting the balloon to the ground. When in order to prevent the young soldier from being dragged into the winch the tether rope was cut, the "balloon bounded two miles into the air. First it drifted over the Union lines, then was blown back toward the Confederate lines near Yorktown. The Confederates, seeing it coming from that direction, promptly opened fire. Finally it skimmed the surface of the York River, its guide-rope splashing in the water, and landed in an orchard. On this trip the balloon made a half-moon circuit of about fifteen miles, about four miles of which was over the York River."*

*The Photographic History of the Civil War, Francis Trevelyan Miller, editor-in-chief, New York: The Review of Reviews Co., 1911

THE NATIONAL AIR AND SPACE MUSEUM
VOLUME ONE • AIR
A Bantam Book/published by arrangement with
Harry N. Abrams Inc.

PRINTING HISTORY
Abrams edition published September 1979
A Selection of Book-of-the-Month Club, Spring 1980
Bantam edition/October 1982
All rights reserved.
Copyright © 1979, 1982 by The Smithsonian Institution.

This book may not be reproduced in whole or in part, by mimeograph or any other means, without permission. For information address: Harry N. Abrams Inc., Subs. of The Times Mirror Co., 110 E. 59th Street, New York, N.Y. 10022

Project Editor: Edith M. Pavese
Assistant Editor: Margaret Donovan
Design Copyright © 1979, 1982 by
David Larkin, Becontree Press

Library of Congress Cataloging in Publication Data

Bryan, Courtlandt Dixon Barnes.
    National Air and Space Museum. Volume One, Air.
    Includes index.
    1. National Air and Space Museum.   I. Title.
TL506.U6W373   629.1′074′0153   79-1432
ISBN 0-553-01384-X

Published simultaneously in the United States and Canada

Bantam Books are published by Bantam Books, Inc. Its trademark, consisting of the words "Bantam Books" and the portrayal of a rooster, is Registered in U.S. Patent and Trademark Office and in other countries. Marca Registrada. Bantam Books, Inc., 666 Fifth Avenue, New York, New York 10103.

Grateful acknowledgment is made for permission to quote from the following works:

Oral Histories from the Oral History Research Office, Columbia University, (Lt. Macready) Copyright 1974, (Lt. Leslie P. Arnold) Copyright 1979, and (Frank Coffyn) Copyright 1979 by the Trustees of Columbia University and The City of New York.

The Washington Post, June 27, 1976. Copyright © 1976 The Washington Post.

MAN AND SPACE, a volume of Life Science Library, by Arthur C. Clarke and the Editors of Time-Life Books, Copyright 1964 and 1969 Time, Inc.

WE SEVEN, BY THE ASTRONAUTS THEMSELVES by M. Scott Carpenter, Copyright 1962 by Simon & Schuster, Inc., by permission of Simon & Schuster, a Division of Gulf & Western Corporation.

CARRYING THE FIRE by Michael Collins, Copyright © 1974 by Michael Collins, by permission of Farrar, Straus & Giroux, Inc.

FIRST ON THE MOON by Neil Armstrong, Michael Collins, Edwin E. Aldrin, Jr., with Gene Farmer and Dora Jane Hamblin, Copyright © 1970 by Little Brown & Co., by permission of the publisher.

The London Economist, July 26, 1969, Copyright 1969 by The Economist Newspaper Ltd., London.

A HOUSE IN SPACE by Henry S. F. Cooper, Jr., Copyright 1976 by Henry S.F. Cooper, Jr. Reprinted by permission of Holt, Rinehart and Winston, Publishers.

The National Geographic Magazine, Vol. 160, No. 4, October 1981. "Our Phenomenal First Flight" by John Young and Robert Crippen.

PRINTED IN THE UNITED STATES OF AMERICA

0 9 8 7 6 5 4 3 2 1

Contents

The school buses, tour buses, charter buses begin lining up along Jefferson Drive on the Mall side of the Smithsonian Institution's National Air and Space Museum (NASM) in Washington, D.C., a half hour before the doors to the huge pink marble and glass sheathed building even open. Early visitors push eagerly forward, crowd against the immense Milestones of Flight gallery windows, shield their eyes and press their foreheads to the glass to peer inside. They point, glance away for but an instant to talk excitedly among themselves, then quickly turn back to look inside again.

Neither the visitor's age nor his nationality seems to matter, his eyes always reflect the excitement, the anticipation, the wonder of a child; and it is exactly this joyful expectancy one sees on the Museum visitor's face that provides the most dramatic evidence of the National Air and Space Museum's enormous popularity—a popularity measured by the fact that more people visit NASM than the Lincoln Memorial, the Washington Monument, the United States Capitol, and the White House *combined.*

Each person who visits the National Air and Space Museum finds himself affected personally by the sudden, unexpected intimacy of his contact with history—history which, in some cases, is so recent that it is not surprising when a Museum visitor is seen reaching hesitantly upward toward a spacecraft's heat shield as if it might still be warm to the touch. And each visitor comes away from the Museum with a sense of awe, for nowhere else in the world has been gathered such overwhelming proof that some of our most elemental dreams can and do come true. But, what is so astonishing, perhaps, is that so many of these dreams came true so fast.

Only twenty-four years after Orville Wright skimmed above the Kill Devil Hill's sands for one hundred and twenty feet in twelve seconds that cold, windy December day near Kitty Hawk in 1903, Charles A. Lindbergh flew his Ryan monoplane, the *Spirit of St. Louis,* alone for 3,610 miles in 33 hours and 30 minutes non-stop across the Atlantic.

Orville Wright was still alive on October 14, 1947, when Charles Yeager in the Bell X-1 became the first man to break the speed of sound. And less than thirteen years later on February 20, 1962, John Glenn became the first American to orbit the earth.

In his Mercury spacecraft, *Friendship 7,* Glenn traveled 80,428 miles at 17,500 mph and within 4 hours and 55 minutes three times circled the earth at an altitude between 101 and 162 miles. The first liquid-propellant rocket had been developed by Robert H. Goddard only thirty-six years before; the Goddard 1926 rocket had reached an altitude of 41 feet in 2.5 seconds.

In July, 1969, only sixty-five years and seven months after the Wright brothers' Flyer became the world's first powered airplane to carry a man and fly under control, astronauts Neil Armstrong, Edwin Aldrin, and Michael Collins rocketed to the Moon in the Apollo 11 spacecraft and while Collins circled above in the command module *Columbia,* Armstrong and Aldrin dropped down to the surface in the lunar module and became the first men to walk upon the Moon.

The Wright Flyer, Lindbergh's *Spirit of St. Louis,* Yeager's Bell X-1, Goddard's 1926 rocket, Glenn's *Friendship 7,* Armstrong, Aldrin, and Collins' Apollo 11 command module *Columbia* are all there in the National Air and Space Museum's Milestones of Flight gallery. Small wonder that those early visitors waiting for the Museum's doors to open peer so eagerly through the glass; they are looking upon treasures more fabulous than any Pharaoh's fortune.

Congress established the National Air Museum on August 12, 1946, as a Smithsonian bureau to "memorialize the national development of aviation; collect, preserve, and display aeronautical equipment of historic interest and significance; serve as a repository for scientific equipment and data pertaining to the development of aviation; and provide educational material for the historical study of aviation." (Twenty years later that act of Congress was amended to include space

The pilot lay prone in the Wright Flyer (1903).

flight.) Recognizing that before NASM could fulfill its mandate, a new museum building would be essential, Congress in 1958 designated the present site for the new National Air and Space Museum which officially opened to the public on July 1, 1976.

The goal of the Museum has been to present the story of flight in all its dimensions. And fundamentally, like other museums, NASM uses words, images, and physical objects to communicate with the visitor. The basic organization of the galleries is uncomplicated; each is devoted to a single subject or theme so that when taken in totality they do cover the entire concept of flight. The Museum's main objectives have been communication of information and feeling and its exhibits have been aimed at making the visitor a willing and happy participant in the process. And there is the key to the Museum's popularity. Visitors are *urged* to have fun, to stand in the cockpit of a DC-7, to walk through a Skylab Orbital Workshop, to touch a piece of the Moon. In the Sea-Air Operations gallery the visitor stands on an aircraft carrier's "hangar deck" among actual Navy fighter planes and bombers. In the World War I Aviation gallery the visitor is "transported" to an Allied advance air base just two days before the end of the war.

All of the airplanes exhibited are genuine. The spacecraft are the actual craft used if they were returned from space. (If the return was not possible, NASM exhibits the real back-up vehicle or a replica made from actual flight hardware.) The Apollo 11 command module *Columbia* is the very one in which Neil Armstrong, Edwin Aldrin, and Michael Collins returned from the Moon.

This book is an attempt to recapture some of the National Air and Space Museum experience. Wherever possible we have supplemented the text with the personal reminiscences, eyewitness accounts, actual logs, or written records of some of the men who designed or flew in the machines on exhibit. We hope thereby to provide the Museum visitor and reader of this book with an even deeper understanding and appreciation of the wonders of flight. And though the objects exhibited in the Museum can be admired for their uncanny sculptural beauty, and the sometimes marvelous functions they have performed, one must never lose sight of the fact that they are only the footprints left behind by humanity on its arduous, occasionally halting but wholly satisfactory, admirable, and inevitable journey to the stars.

Milestones of Flight

Among its cast of out-and-out cranks and eccentrics, every small town in turn-of-the-Century America had its two or three inventors, tinkerers, men who believed their better mousetrap, their superior tool, their perpetual-motion machine would—after just a little more refinement—bring them fortune and fame. For them Thomas Edison epitomized the belief that by inventing something they would turn themselves into tycoons. Two such men were Orville and Wilbur Wright, whose unstinting patience, scientific intuition, methodical experimentation, and boundless confidence and optimism enabled them within four years to succeed in resolving and providing satisfactory solutions to the seemingly insurmountable problems that had plagued all their predecessors and prevented men from achieving winged, powered, controlled flight.

Wilbur Wright was born in Millville, Indiana, on April 16, 1867, the year Dr. David Livingstone was exploring the Congo in search of the source of the Nile.

Orville Wright was born in Dayton, Ohio, four years later, on August 19, 1871, the year New York *Herald* reporter Henry M. Stanley greeted a stooped and sickly white man at Ujiji, Central Africa, saying, "Dr. Livingstone, I presume?"

To set the Wright brothers in time is easy enough, but to separate the reality of their personalities from the portraits painted of them over the years by myth, malice, and misunderstanding is more difficult. C. H. Gibbs-Smith, the Smithsonian's first Lindbergh Professor of Aerospace History, has long fought attempts to depict the Wrights as a couple of bright, local boys who "with wire, spit, sticks, canvas, and spare parts from their bicycle shop put together an airplane."

The Wrights, he has said, "were among the best educated men in the United States in the 19th Century." Although neither Wilbur nor Orville bothered to graduate from high school one has only to dip into their correspondence or attempt to follow their technical and theoretical experiments to realize the high quality of education they achieved.

When, in 1895, the Wright brothers read of the gliding experiments being conducted by Otto Lilienthal, Germany's first and foremost contributor to the conquest of the air, they sought every piece of information they could learn about him. Between 1891 and 1896 Lilienthal had made over 2,000 glides—some of them several hundred feet—down a large hill he had constructed near Berlin. His early gliders were monoplanes with fixed tails. The pilot's head and shoulders were above the cambered wings, his hips and legs dangled below. What limited directional control Lilienthal achieved he managed by shifting his hips and weight from side to side or back and forth. Photographs and published reports of Lilienthal's experiments fascinated the Wrights. He had effectively demonstrated that air *could* support a man in winged flight.

Ever since 1891 Lilienthal had been designing and constructing gliders with the hope that when a suitable means of propulsion was developed, it could be added to his wings. In 1896 he had built a glider with flapping wing tips powered by a small compressed carbonic acid gas motor. Unfortunately, before Lilienthal had an opportunity to test it, he was killed in one of his standard gliders when a sudden gust of wind forced the glider upward into a stall. The craft crashed to earth and broke the aviation pioneer's back. He died the next day. One of Lilienthal's gliders can be seen at the entrance to the Early Flight gallery on the first floor. Lilienthal's death made the Wrights only more eager to learn not only everything he had accomplished, but what progress others as well had made toward achieving human flight. In 1899, aware of the aeronautical studies and experiments being conducted by Dr. Samuel P. Langley, the third Secretary of the Smithsonian Institution, Wilbur Wright wrote the Institution:

> I have been interested in the problem of mechanical and human flight ever since as a boy I constructed a number of bats [Wilbur's name for helicopter models] of various sizes after the style of Cayley's and Pénaud's machines. My observations since have only convinced me more firmly that human flight is possible and practicable. It is only a question of knowledge and skill just as in all acrobatic feats . . . .
>
> I am about to begin a systematic study of the subject in preparation for practical work to which I expect to devote what time I can spare from my regular business. I am an enthusiast, but not a crank in the sense that I have some pet theories as to the proper construction of a flying machine, I wish to avail myself of all that is already known and then if possible add my mite to help on the future worker who will attain final success.

The Smithsonian responded by suggesting that the Wrights read Octave Chanute's *Progress in Flying Machines,* Professor Langley's *Experiments in Aerodynamics,* and the Aeronautical Annuals of 1895-97 containing reprints of accounts of experiments going back to the 15th Century. The Smithsonian also sent pamphlets containing material extracted from the Institution's own reports. The Wrights read them eagerly and were surprised to learn how much time and money had already been spent attempting to solve the problem of human flight; they were perhaps even more astonished by the caliber of the men who had tried. Among them were such men as Leonardo da Vinci; Sir George Cayley, designer (in 1799) of the first modern configuration airplane; Professor Langley, Secretary and head of the Smithsonian

Institution; Dr. Alexander Graham Bell, inventor of the telephone; Sir Hiram Maxim, inventor of the automatic gun; Mr. O. Chanute, the past president of the American Society of Civil Engineers; Mr. Chas. Parsons, the inventor of the steam turbine; Mr. Thomas A. Edison; Herr Lilienthal and a host of others.

One by one these men had been beaten and discontinued their efforts. Rather than being discouraged by their predecessors' failures, the Wrights plunged ahead and a mere three months after they had received the pamphlets from the Smithsonian they had constructed their first aircraft, a biplane kite with a five-foot wingspan and a fixed horizontal tailplane. This craft incorporated what Gibbs-Smith describes as "their first decisive discovery and first decisive invention": wing warping.

"The Wrights had observed that gliding and soaring birds," Professor Gibbs-Smith writes, "evidenced especially by their local 'expert' the buzzard 'regain their lateral balance when partly overturned by a gust of wind, by a torsion of the tips of the wings. If the rear edge of the right wing is twisted upward and the left downward the bird . . . instantly begins to turn, a line from its head to its tail being the axis. It thus regains its level even if thrown on its beam's end, so to speak, as I have frequently seen them,'* and [the Wrights] decided to apply this bird practice to aeroplane wings . . . ."

Anyone attempting to attain sustained powered flight, the Wrights realized, was confronted with three problems: the first was the design and construction of a device capable of remaining with a man in the air; the second was finding how to control the device once it was up in the air; the third problem was that once one had a device that could remain with a man in the air and under control, one still had to provide a safe, practical propulsion system to keep him up there. The Wrights' No. 1 Glider, completed in

---

*Prof. Gibbs-Smith is quoting here from a letter written by Orville to Octave Chanute on May 13, 1900.

The Wright Flyer in which, on December 17, 1903, one of man's oldest dreams was realized when Orville Wright achieved the world's first successful controlled, powered, manned, heavier-than-air flight. His epoch-making 120-foot journey lasted just 12 seconds, but aviation was born.

September, 1900, was a biplane weighing about 52 pounds, with a wingspan of a little over 17 feet and a total lifting area of only 165 square feet. There was no tail unit, and the wing-warping cables could be worked either by the operator or from the ground.

Aware that their first full-size glider was in essence a big kite and that a strong wind would be required to keep it aloft, the Wrights wrote the Weather Service in Washington to learn where suitable winds might be found. The closest site to Dayton was to the east at a desolate, isolated spot along North Carolina's coast: Kitty Hawk.

Wilbur Wright wrote to his father:

September 3, 1900

I am intending to start in a few days for a trip to the coast of North Carolina . . . for the purpose of making some experiments with a flying machine. It is my belief that flight is possible and, while I am taking up the investigation for pleasure rather than profit, I think there is a slight possibility of achieving fame and fortune from it . . . .

The Wright No. 1 Glider had two important basic control elements: the first was a "horizontal rudder" (or elevator) placed about 30 inches in front of the leading edge of the lower wing. The Wrights believed that by placing the elevator in front rather than behind the wings they would provide themselves with a safer fore-and-aft balance control, especially should a sudden downdraft force the craft to drop. The second element was, of course, the wing warping. However, due to the small lifting area of the glider's wings, they had to fly it chiefly as a kite.

By the end of that season's experiments the Wrights had flown their No. 1 Glider manned just ten minutes as a kite, and had acquired only two minutes of actual gliding time. Still, the Wrights were not discouraged; they had proved that their wing-warping method for achieving lateral control worked more successfully than any method previously attempted, and their front elevator had also provided the most successful means of vertical control.

The Wrights' No. 2 Glider was brought to Kill Devil Hill, four miles south of Kitty Hawk, in July, 1901. (The Wrights never did use Kitty Hawk except for their tests with their No. 1 Glider, preferring instead the Kill Devil Hill site.) Glider No. 2 was a larger machine than anyone had attempted to fly before and too large to be controlled simply by an operator shifting his weight. Its 22-foot wingspan provided a lifting area of 290 square feet. Since the glider had been designed to fly in winds of at least 17 mph and the winds on July 27, the day the Wrights were ready to test it, never reached more than 14 mph, they carried the glider to the top of Kill Devil Hill for its first trial. They made five or six brief "tuning up" flights, then made a glide that lasted 19 seconds and covered 315 feet. Although several of their flights on the first day exceeded the best of those made in the No. 1 Glider the previous year, the Wrights realized that in some ways their new glider was not as good, and that in particular it could not glide at a slope nearly as level as the 1900 machine had achieved. Wilbur noted in his diary:

July 30, 1901

The most discouraging features of our experiments so far are these: the lift is not much over one third that indicated by the Lilienthal tables.

The absolute faith the Wrights had had in the scientific data compiled by their predecessors, Lilienthal especially, was badly shaken. It was becoming obvious that the center of pressure on a curved or cambered surface did not—as all the scientific books taught—travel in the same direction as it would on a plane surface, and that, in fact, the center of pressure appeared to reverse once a certain angle of attack was achieved. Wilbur was so discouraged that on their way back to Dayton he said, "Not within a thousand years will man ever fly." Orville argued that the unreliability of their predecessors' work did not mean that flight was impossible, it meant only that more knowledge and effort were necessary.

Out of an old starch box Orville constructed a small wind tunnel and one day's tests were enough to show them that all the existing scientific tables regarding the effect of air pressure on airplane surfaces contained serious errors. They constructed a larger, more sophisticated wind tunnel: a wooden box 16 inches square inside and 6 feet long. During that autumn and winter of 1901, a span of just over two months, the Wrights tested a little over two hundred different types of wing surfaces in their wind tunnel. They tried monoplane, biplane, and triplane configurations in addition to models with two wings placed on the same level, one behind the other, as Langley had done.

The Wrights finally decided they would have to test their newly acquired knowledge with a third glider at Kill Devil Hill. Their No. 3 Glider was ready for its first trial on September 29, 1902. The No. 3 Glider's lifting area was not that much greater than that of No. 2 (305 square feet *vs.* 290 square feet). The No. 3 Glider's wings were longer and narrower than those of No. 2. Wing-warping controls were linked to the "cradle" in which the operator's hips rested and to

warp the wings the pilot simply shifted his hips from side to side. The most visible change was the addition of a tail consisting of two fixed vertical fins.

The first trials with the No. 3 Glider were encouraging. The Wrights, that September and October of 1902, made over a thousand glides—the longest was 622½ feet, and the greatest duration was 22½ seconds—and a number of them were made against a 36 mile per hour wind, stiffer than any previous glider experimenter had attempted. Still, about once in every fifty glides in spite of all the warp the pilot could give to the wing tips the machine would turn up sideways in a bank and slip down to the ground. Nothing like this had occurred with their previous gliders and so the brothers deduced that whatever was happening was being caused by the addition of the tail.

When the Wrights returned to work on the No. 3 Glider they attached the wires controlling the rudder to those warping the wings; further, they changed the two vertical surfaces on the rudder to one single vertical fin.

Glider pioneer Otto Lilienthal achieved control by shifting his weight.

An original Lilienthal Standard glider similar to the type in which its inventor lost his life.

With the movable tail the Wrights had created a practical glider so efficient it broke all existing records: it was the largest machine (32 foot 1 inch wingspan), capable of the longest time in the air (26 seconds) and covering the greatest distance (622½ feet) with the smallest angle of descent (5 degrees)—an angle less than could be attained by any of the hawks they had so carefully observed—and it had been flown in higher winds than anyone had hitherto attempted (36 mph).

Because of the triumphant success of their No. 3 Glider, the Wrights were convinced they could now build a successful *powered* aircraft.

There were two monumental obstacles the Wrights still had to overcome: they had to acquire an engine capable of producing at least 8 horsepower that would weigh no more than 200 pounds; and second, they would need propellers.

In an attempt to surmount the first obstacle the Wrights, in December, 1902, wrote to a number of automobile companies and gasoline-engine manufacturers asking whether they had a motor that fulfilled their requirements. None did—or if they did, they were hesitant to provide one for anything so lunatic as powering a "flying machine"—and so Wilbur and Orville, with the help of Charles Taylor, their bicycle assistant, designed and built one themselves. An even more formidable task was designing the propellers.

The Wrights had not anticipated the almost total lack of scientific knowledge about the workings and design of propellers that existed; after all, the screw propeller had been in use on ships for nearly a century. When they finished their reading they realized that all the formulas on the action of propellers in water had been arrived at through trial and error rather than through any scientific theory. Rough estimates might do for a motorboat since a propeller operating at less than the desired efficiency would still move the boat forward a little. But unless a propeller on a flying machine provided the necessary thrust, the machine would not fly.

It took months for the Wrights to reduce their theories into formulas, to learn enough about propellers to be able to calculate how specific designs would work.

Not until late September were the Wrights prepared to leave for the North Carolina coast. Their previous year's camp at Kill Devil Hill had been blown off its foundations by a storm; they repaired the damage and built a second shed to house both the No. 3 Glider (1902) and the new powered machine with which they confidently expected to fly.

During this time, Samuel Pierpont Langley, the distinguished Secretary of the Smithsonian Institution, was readying his "aerodrome" for launch from a houseboat on Washington's Potomac River. Langley's "aerodrome" was a gasoline-engine-powered aircraft with two main wings with a span of 48 feet 5 inches placed in tandem, one behind the other, with a stabilizer and tail behind. Seven years earlier, on May 6, 1896, Langley had achieved the distinction of launching the first American heavier-than-air flying machine capable of making a free flight of any significant length. The machine Langley's Aerodrome #5, was a model, unmanned of course, and it flew about 3,000 feet at about 25 mph. On October 7, 1903, with his gifted assistant Charles M. Manly at the controls (and with a compass optimistically sewn onto the knee of Manly's trousers), Langley prepared for what with reasonable confidence he believed would be the first man-carrying powered heavier-than-air flying machine's flight in history. At noon that day the 52-horsepower, gasoline-powered five-cylinder radial engine was started and the twin propellers flung back the air. Langley's tandem-winged "aerodrome" shuddered upon its catapult atop the Potomac River houseboat like a beast straining to be free and then, according to the Washington *Post* this is what happened:

When Langley's aerodrome was catapult-launched

from atop a Potomac River houseboat it

"simply slid into the water like a handful of mortar..."

. . . A few yards from the houseboat were the boats of the reporters, who for three months had been stationed at Widewater [waiting for the flight to be attempted]. The newspapermen waved their hands. Manly looked down and smiled. Then his face hardened as he braced himself for the flight, which might have in store for him fame or death. The propeller wheels, a foot from his head, whirred around him one thousand times to the minute. A man forward fired two sky rockets. There came an answering 'toot, toot,' from the tugs. A mechanic stooped, cut the cable holding the catapult; there was a roaring, grinding noise—and the Langley airship tumbled over the edge of the houseboat and disappeared in the river, sixteen feet below. It simply slid into the water like a handful of mortar . . .

—Washington *Post*, Oct. 8, 1903

On December 8th, Langley prepared for another attempt. His "aerodrome" had been pulled out of the Potomac River and repaired. Convinced that his previous failure had been due to some part of his machine's structure becoming fouled in the catapult rather than any problem with the design of his craft itself, he ignored the catcalls and criticism of the press and prepared to catapult-launch his "aerodrome" again. There exists a photograph of the result: the "aerodrome" with pilot Manly sitting stoic and erect in the cockpit has just been launched. The nose of the aircraft is pointing straight up; everything aft of Manly and the spinning propellers is falling apart. The forward set of tandem wings appears reasonably solid still, but the second set has crumpled upward like hands clasping in prayer. One can make out broken spars, tearing canvas, bits of debris dropping into the water; the edge of the houseboat remains in view. Manly, unhurt, was once again pulled dripping out of the river; Langley's spirit, however, was crushed by the resulting brutal attacks of the press and by what one writer has referred to as "the curious sadism with which crowds had greeted aeronautical failures since the days of the Montgolfiers."

On Monday, December 14th, six days after Langley's failure, the Wrights prepared to fly. Like Langley's machine the Wrights' "Flyer"

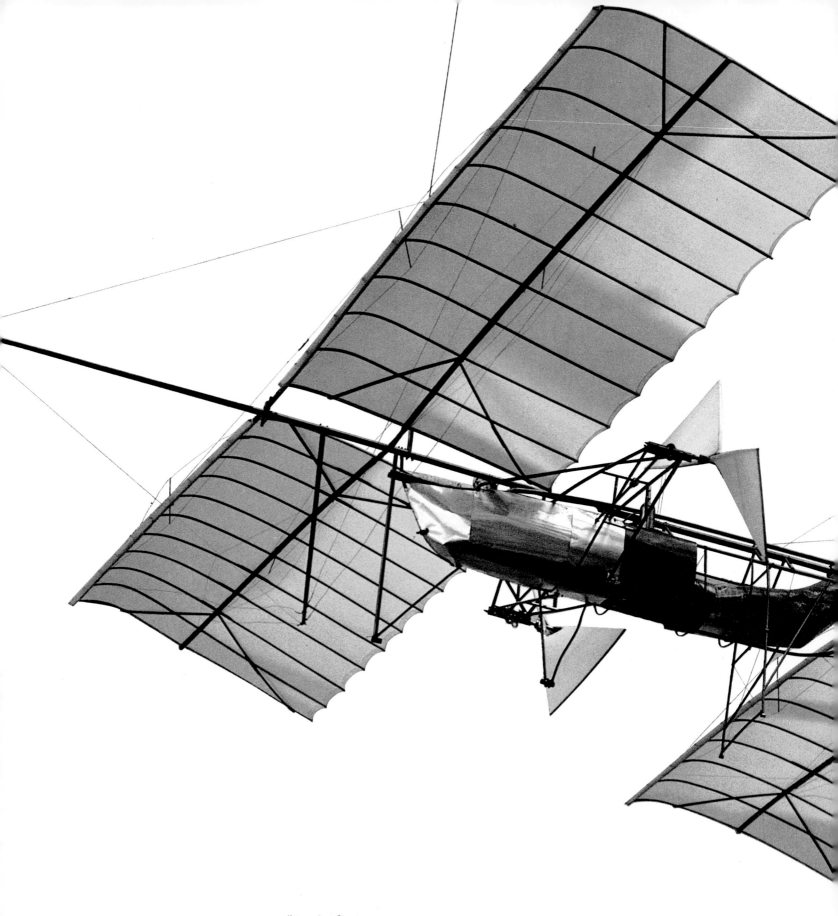

The 1896 Langley Aerodrome #5—the first American powered, heavier-than-air machine to make a flight of significant length.

(the name they gave all their powered machines) had twin propellers. The propellers' counter-rotation, the Wrights hoped, would neutralize any gyroscopic torque; in addition, two propellers would react against a greater quantity of air. Like their earlier gliders, the first Wright Flyer was a biplane with a skid undercarriage; but it was a considerable machine: its wingspan had been increased to 40 feet 4 inches with a wing area of 510 square feet.

The Wrights did not use any weights or derrick device to launch it; instead, the craft's undercarriage skids rested on a 6-foot-long plank which, in turn, was laid across a smaller piece of wood to which had been attached two modified bicycle wheel hubs one in front of the other. These two hubs had ball bearings and flanges to prevent them from slipping off the 60-foot-long launching track. The track was nothing more than a series of two-by-four boards laid on their edges end to end with their upper surface covered by a thin sheet of metal.

On Monday, the wind was too light to launch from level ground and the Wrights knew they would have to transport their Flyer to some lower slopes about a quarter-mile away.

Since obviously both Orville and Wilbur were eager to make the first flight (and since they were both equally experienced pilots by now), they decided a coin toss would determine which of them would go. Wilbur won.

The Flyer's engine was started and permitted to warm up. Then Wilbur climbed onto the machine, and settled himself into the prone position with his hips in the "cradle" to control the rudder and warp. Orville took up his position at a wing tip to help balance the machine as it gathered speed down the track. Wilbur glanced at Orville, nodded that he was ready, then he slipped the restraining wire, and the Wright Flyer took off down the rail so fast Orville couldn't keep up.

Wilbur wrote his family that night:

We gave machine first trial today with only partial success . . . . The wind was a little to one side, and the track was not exactly straight down hill, which caused the start to be more difficult than it would otherwise have been. However, the real trouble was an error in judgment in turning up too suddenly after leaving the track, and as the machine had barely speed enough for support already, this slowed it down so much that before I could correct the error, the machine began to come down, though turned up at a big angle.

Toward the end it began to speed up again but it was too late and it struck the ground while moving a little to one side, due to wind and a rather bad start. A few sticks in the front rudder were broken.

It took almost two days to repair the damage to the Flyer's rudder, and the machine was not ready until too late in the afternoon of December 16 to fly. A strong, cold northerly wind blew in overnight and by the next morning puddles of water about their camp were covered with a thin skim of ice. The wind continued at about 25 mph during the early morning, and the Wrights retired indoors to wait for the wind to die down and for themselves to warm up. But when, at ten o'clock, the wind had still not diminished, the Wrights made up their minds to take the machine out anyway and attempt a flight. Although they were aware of the risk in flying in so strong a wind, they believed that the potential for danger would be compensated for by the slower speed in landing. Because Wilbur had won the first toss, it was now Orville's turn to attempt the flight. Before climbing onto the Flyer, Orville set his camera on a tripod and aimed its lens at a specific point about two-thirds down the 60-foot track, the spot where Orville fully expected the machine to become airborne. He asked J. T. Daniels of the Life-Saving Station to be the photographer. "When I turn the wings to a flying angle," Orville told him, "I'll leave the track and should be about two feet off the ground when directly in front of the camera. That's the time to press the button." And then, satisfied that Daniels understood him,* Orville joined Wilbur and they started the Flyer's engine. Let Orville's diary tell the story:

Thursday, December 17, 1903
After running the engine and propellers a few minutes to get them in working order, I got on the machine at 10:35 for the first trial. . . . On slipping the rope the machine started off increasing in speed to probably 7 or 8 miles. The machine lifted from the track just as it was entering on the fourth rail. . . .

I found the control of the front rudder [elevator] quite difficult on account of its being balanced too near the center and thus had a tendency to turn itself when started so that the rudder was turned too far on one side and then too far on the other. As a result the machine would rise suddenly to about 10 feet and then as suddenly, on turning the rudder, dart for the ground. A sudden dart when out about 100 feet from the end of the track ended the flight. Time about 12 seconds (not known exactly as watch was not properly stopped). The flight lever for throwing off the engine was broken, and the skid under the rudder cracked.

*The photograph later developed in Dayton turned out precisely balanced just as Orville had expected and is, in its own way, as perfect an example of the Wrights' careful and methodical preparation having led to success as the flight itself. In the photograph one can see the elevator straining upward, the Flyer piloted by Orville skimming about two feet above the track and Wilbur, no longer needing to balance the wing tip, falling away from their machine with a mixture of wonder and awe at the triumph they had achieved.

The nose of the Spirit of St. Louis wears the flags of the United States, France, Belgium, England, Mexico and other Latin American countries, and the islands of the West Indies that Lindbergh and his Ryan aircraft visited.

It is not surprising that whoever was holding the stopwatch failed to promptly mark the time—he was witnessing the first time in history that a man-carrying machine had lifted itself into the air under its own power, had sailed forward without slowing, and had landed on ground as high as that from which it had taken off.

Orville's diary:

After repairs, at 20 minutes after 11 o'clock Will made the second trial. The course was about like mine, up and down but a little longer . . . over the ground though about the same in time. Distance not measured but about 175 feet. Wind speed not quite so strong.

With the aid of the station men present, we picked the machine up and carried it back to the starting ways. At about 20 minutes till 12 o'clock I made the third trial. When out about the same distance as Will's, I met with a strong gust from the left which raised the left wing and sidled the machine off to the right in a lively manner. I immediately turned the rudder to bring the machine down and then worked the end control. Much to our surprise, on reaching the ground the left wing struck first, showing the lateral control of this machine much more effective than on any of our former ones. At the time of its sidling it had raised to a height of probably 12 to 14 feet.

At just 12 o'clock Will started on the fourth and last trip. The machine started off with its ups and downs as it had before, but by the time he had gone three or four hundred feet he had it under much better control, and was traveling on a fairly even course. It proceeded in this manner till it reached a small hummock out about 800 feet from the starting ways, when it began its pitching again and suddenly darted into the ground. The front rudder frame was badly broken up, but the main frame suffered none at all. The distance over the ground was 852 feet in 59 seconds . . . .

After removing the front rudder, we carried the machine back to camp. We set the machine down a few feet west of the building, and while standing about discussing the last flight, a sudden gust of wind struck the machine and started to turn it over. All rushed to stop it. Will, who was near the end, ran to the front, but too late to do any good . . . . The machine gradually turned over on us.

The engine legs were all broken off, the chain guides badly bent, a number of uprights, and nearly all the rear ends of the ribs were broken. One spar only was broken . . . .

All possibility of further flights with the machine for that year had ended.

Curiously, despite the historic significance of what the brothers had accomplished, there does not appear to have been any sense of excitement at their camp that day, least of all shown by Wilbur and Orville themselves.

After surveying the damage done to their Flyer, Orville and Wilbur went into their camp building, prepared and ate their lunch, and then after washing their dishes and putting them away, they walked the four or so miles to the Kitty Hawk Weather Station, where they could send a telegram to their father. While Wilbur was examining the machine that recorded the wind velocity, Orville sent the following message: SUCCESS FOUR FLIGHTS THURSDAY MORNING ALL AGAINST TWENTY-ONE MILE WIND STARTED FROM LEVEL WITH ENGINE POWER ALONE AVERAGE SPEED THROUGH AIR THIRTY-ONE MILES LONGEST 59 SECONDS INFORM PRESS HOME CHRISTMAS. ORVILLE WRIGHT.

There had been a flight.

And the world would never be the same.

Stand in the center of the vast Milestones of Flight gallery and look again at that fragile, austere, antique Wright Flyer suspended overhead, then look down at the sweep secondhand of your wristwatch and count off twelve seconds, twelve engine-popping, chain-rattling seconds of uneven darting flight and that is all the time Wilbur and Orville Wright needed to fulfill one of the earliest dreams of man. Glance up again at the Flyer and pay your respects, but then shift your gaze to the small, silver, high-winged monoplane above the Wright Flyer and to its right. It is the *Spirit of St. Louis* and on May 20-21, 1927, for 33 hours, 30 minutes and 29.8 seconds, it made the most famous flight in history.

The "NYP" below the "Ryan" painted on the
Spirit of St. Louis' tail stood for New York—to—Paris.

On May 22, 1919, Raymond Orteig, a New York hotel owner, offered a $25,000 prize "to the first aviator who shall cross the Atlantic in a land or water aircraft (heavier-than-air) from Paris or the shores of France to New York, or from New York to Paris or the shores of France, without stop." Although this was an era of aircraft speed, distance, and duration record breaking attempts, for the next eight years the Orteig Prize went unclaimed. No one had been able to make the 3,300-mile flight between Paris and New York non-stop because until 1926 there simply did not exist an aircraft engine reliable enough to permit a flight of that duration and distance. But then came the 220-horsepower, aircooled Wright Whirlwind engine produced by Charles L. Lawrance for the Wright Aeronautical Company.

Charles A. Lindbergh was twenty-four years old and flying the mail in an old DH-4 one moonlit night when it suddenly occurred to him to try for the Orteig Prize. He had more than four years of aviation behind him, close to two thousand hours flying time, had barnstormed over half the then-48 states and flown mail through appalling weather. He had learned the basics of navigation as a flying cadet at Brooks and Kelly Fields. He had the experience; all he lacked was the money. So with $2,000 of his own savings he approached a group of St. Louis businessmen and after convincing them that a flight *was* possible, they agreed to raise an additional $13,000 toward the purchase of a monoplane equipped with one of the new Wright engines.

Lindbergh was by no means alone in

pursuing the Orteig Prize. René Fonck, France's leading World War I ace (75 victories), had attempted the flight in a Sikorsky tri-motor. The heavily fuel-laden aircraft's landing gear had buckled on take-off from Long Island's Roosevelt Field and two of his crew members had perished in the fiery crash. Fokker was building a tri-motor for Commander Richard Byrd's attempt; and the Columbia Aircraft Company was preparing one of Guiseppe Bellanca's stunning Wright-powered monoplanes. Lt. Comdr. Noel Davis and Lt. Stanton Wooster of the U. S. Navy were readying the "American Legion," a large Keystone Pathfinder tri-motor biplane for their flight. French war hero Charles Nungesser and François Coli, on the other side of the Atlantic, were going to try an East-West

crossing in a 450 hp single-engine French-built Levasseur biplane.

Lindbergh and his backers could not afford a Fokker; the Columbia Aircraft Company did not have enough confidence in Lindbergh to offer him their Wright-Bellanca. Other aircraft manufacturers wanted too much money or could not build the plane. Lindbergh turned to the small, relatively unknown Ryan Airlines, Inc., of San Diego, California and on February 24, 1927, Lindbergh wired his backers: BELIEVE RYAN CAPABLE OF BUILDING PLANE WITH SUFFICIENT PERFORMANCE STOP COST COMPLETE WITH WHIRLWIND ENGINE AND STANDARD INSTRUMENTS IS TEN THOUSAND FIVE HUNDRED EIGHTY DOLLARS STOP DELIVERY WITHIN SIXTY DAYS STOP RECOMMEND CLOSING DEAL. LINDBERGH

Sixty days after the contract with Ryan is negotiated, the *Spirit of St. Louis* is flying—but so are the others. On April 16, 1927, Commander Byrd's big Fokker, the *America*, overturns on landing at New York's Teterboro Airport; pilot Floyd Bennett is seriously injured.

On April 24th, the Wright-Bellanca loses a wheel off its landing gear during a test flight and is damaged on landing.

On April 26th, Lt. Comdr. Davis and Lt. Wooster are killed on their last trial flight when their Keystone Pathfinder biplane crashes in a marsh short of the runway at Langley Field.

On May 8th, Nungesser and Coli take off from Le Bourget Field near Paris for New York—and disappear.

Four men dead, three injured, Nungesser and Coli missing—newspaper editors realize the New York-Paris flight is the story of the year.

On May 11th, Lindbergh lands the *Spirit of St. Louis* at New York's Curtiss Field, and an hour later Byrd's now-repaired *America* lands, too. The Wright-Bellanca had arrived before them. The pilots wait for the weather to clear. A week later dense fog still shrouds the coasts of Nova Scotia and Newfoundland and a storm area is developing in the Atlantic off the coast of France. On a rainy Thursday night in New York, May 19th, Lindbergh is on the way to the theater with Dick Blythe, the Wright Aeronautical Company's representative, when he asks Blythe to stop for one more call to the weather bureau. Blythe returns to report the weather over the ocean is clearing. The low pressure area over Newfoundland is receding and a big high is pushing in behind it. "Of course," Blythe tells Lindbergh, "conditions aren't good all along your route. They say it may take another day or two for that." Lindbergh sees a chance to take off at daybreak and cancels the theater to go out to the airfield to check his plane. He does not return to his hotel room until just before midnight. Three hours later, without any sleep, Lindbergh returns to Curtiss Field.

He is told that in spite of the fog at Roosevelt Field where he is scheduled to take off, the high pressure system is still moving in over the north Atlantic and the fog is lifting between New York and Newfoundland. Lindbergh orders the *Spirit of St. Louis* towed through the rain to Roosevelt Field and the fuel tanks topped.

As soon as the *Spirit of St. Louis* is positioned at the end of the Roosevelt Field runway field into the wind, the wind maddeningly shifts 180° to blow over its tail. The runway is rainsoaked and soft. Huge puddles are visible up the field. The *Spirit of St. Louis,* with its three wing tanks and its nose and fuel tanks filled, weighs 5,250 pounds—a thousand pounds more than Lindbergh has attempted to fly it with before. Because of the nose fuel tank he has no forward vision except through a periscope which is useless when the plane's tailskid is resting on the ground. The engine is running 30 rpm too slow; the mechanic says it's the weather, but Lindbergh sees the apprehension in the mechanic's eyes. Ahead, just beyond the mist-shrouded end of the runway, are the telephone wires Lindbergh will have to clear. He buckles his seatbelt, adjusts his goggles over his eyes, nods at the men on either side of the plane and the wheelchocks are pulled. Lindbergh eases the throttle forward and the *Spirit of St. Louis* slowly creeps through the mud. Lindbergh must keep his plane moving absolutely straight or one wheel will dig in, the heavy load will crush the landing gear, which in turn will explode the fuel. The *Spirit of St. Louis* uses up a thousand feet of runway before its tailskid lifts.

The halfway mark streaks past—seconds now to decide—the wrong decision means a crash—I pull the stick back firmly, and—the wheels leave *the ground.* Then I'll get off! The wheels touch again . . . A shallow pool on the runway—water spews up from the tires—hold to center—must keep straight—water drumming on the fabric—the next hop's longer . . . I let the wheels touch once more. Best to have plenty of control with such a load . . . The *Spirit of St. Louis* takes herself off next time—

full flying speed—the controls taut, alive, straining.

—*Spirit of St. Louis,*
Chas. Lindbergh

Lindbergh clears the telephone wires with forty feet to spare. He is on his way to Paris.

It is perhaps difficult for us today to understand what an extraordinary feat Lindbergh accomplished. Thousands of passengers cross the Atlantic non-stop every week and if they tear their eyes away from the pages of their novel or the onboard movie to look out through the double-layered glass window of their jetliner at the sky, they do not consider the risks. Nor do they question for an instant that if the pilot, or more likely some flight attendant, announces their destination is Paris, that this is precisely where they will arrive. But Lindbergh, from the moment on May 20, 1927, when he struggled into the heavy air from that rain-soaked Roosevelt Field and flew alone thirty-three and a half hours to land at Le Bourget outside Paris, touched some responsive chord in the hearts of the world.

There was something about the tininess of Lindbergh's plane against so huge and implacable a foe as the Atlantic Ocean and its storms, something about Lindbergh's shyness and modesty, his aloofness and self-confidence. He had arrived alone at Roosevelt Field with little fanfare and took off alone crossing the vast Atlantic without sleep in terrible cold, sometimes ten feet above the waves, at other times at ten thousand icy feet threading his way at night through the great cliffs of thunderheads towering around him, toward Le Bourget about which he'd only been told, "It's a big airport. You can't miss it. Just fly northeast from the city."

At night over Paris he sees a dark patch on the ground where he thinks Le Bourget ought to be. Lindbergh continues on to be sure, then circles back over the dark patch again. It must be Le Bourget, Lindbergh thinks, but there seem to be thousands of dim lights to one side. Lindbergh descends to a lower altitude, recognizes big hangars, realizes the little lights are automobiles. It *is* Le Bourget! Lindbergh banks around for his final glide.

I'm too high—too fast. Drop wing—left rudder—sideslip . . . Careful—mustn't stall. I've never landed the *Spirit of St. Louis* at night before. It would be better to come in straight. But if I don't sideslip, I'll be too high over the boundary to touch my wheels in the area of light . . . Still too high. I push the stick over . . . A short burst of the engine—over the lighted area . . . Sod coming up to meet me—Careful—easy to bounce when you're tired . . . Still too fast—Hold off—Hold off . . . The surface dims. Texture of sod is gone—ahead there's nothing but night . . . The wheels touch gently—off again—No, I'll keep contact—Ease the stick forward—Back on the ground—Off—Back—The tailskid, too—Not a bad landing, but I'm beyond the light—Can't see anything ahead—Wish I had a wing light, but too heavy—Slower, now—Slow enough to ground loop safely—left rudder—reverse it—stick over the other way—The *Spirit of St. Louis* swings around and stops rolling resting on the solidness of earth, in the center of Le Bourget. I start to taxi back toward the floodlights and hangars—But the entire field ahead is covered with running figures!

—*Spirit of St. Louis,*
by Chas. Lindbergh

Lindbergh barely has time to stop the engine before the first faces are at the side windows of his silver plane. He hears them shouting LINDBERGH! LINDBERGH! The *Spirit of St. Louis* trembles as bodies crush against it. Souvenir hunters tear pieces of fabric from the fuselage. Lindbergh is pulled bodily out of his plane and carried in triumph over the crowd's heads. Lindbergh had done it *alone*!

And from the night he landed at Le Bourget Lindbergh fought in vain to keep this sense of self intact. Look again at that tiny, silver plane. Charles Lindbergh's *Spirit of St. Louis* holds a very special place in every Museum visitor's heart.

The young Lindbergh in front of the Spirit of
St. Louis' *dependable Wright Whirlwind 220-
hp engine.*

Pioneers of Flight

Museum visitors will often climb up to the balcony above the Milestones of Flight gallery where they can look through the open door of Lindbergh's *Spirit of St. Louis* into the cockpit at the panel whose instruments, Lindbergh wrote, during the long night of flight "stare at me with cold, ghostlike eyes." But then the visitor will turn back, drawn by the very special aircraft that are a part of the Pioneers of Flight gallery. And although the visitor cannot help being drawn to the larger planes in this exhibit, no one who spends any time in this gallery emerges without a very special affection for that frail, canvas-covered Wright EX biplane, the *Vin Fiz*. It was in this machine that Calbraith Perry Rodgers completed the first transcontinental flight while attempting to win William Randolph Hearst's $50,000 prize offered to that person who completed the first coast-to-coast trip in thirty days.

Cal Rodgers, a tall, wiry, cigar-chomping, motorcycle-racing, daredevil descendant of two Naval heroes, had less than sixty hours total flying experience when, on September 17, 1911, he took off from Sheepshead Bay, Brooklyn, in the *Vin Fiz* on the first leg of his trip. He flew to Middleton, New York, where he landed and spent the night. The next morning he took off again and flew directly into a tree, damaging his aircraft so badly it

took three days for it to be repaired. (During a demonstration flight at Fort Myer, a Wright 1909 Military Flyer hit a tree, but it took only four *hours* for its damage to be repaired.) Rodgers' attempt at the Hearst prize was sponsored by the Armour Company which, at that time, was manufacturing a grape-flavored soft drink called "Vin Fiz." Rodgers was paid $5.00 for every mile he flew with the Armour Company's soft drink's name emblazoned on his wing. When the *Vin Fiz* was repaired, Rodgers pushed stubbornly west, followed and occasionally led by a special three-car train carrying his wife, his mother, mechanics, some Armour representatives, and $4,000 worth of spare parts. Rodgers navigated using "the iron compass" (railroad tracks) whenever possible, but because he followed the wrong switch he once ended up in Scranton, Pennsylvania, rather than, as he had intended, Elmira, New York. During his leapfrog journey across the country Rodgers made sixty-nine stops—not all of them intentional. He crashed sixteen times, once suffered an in-flight run-in with an eagle, and his *Vin Fiz* was wrecked so many times that when he finally arrived in California enough spare parts had been used to completely build four planes, and the only pieces that remained of the original *Vin Fiz* in which he had taken off from Sheepshead

Bay were the rudder and two struts from the wing. Rodgers, himself, finished the flight with his leg in a cast and an ugly scar on his forehead. Cal Rodgers did not win the Hearst prize; he had, in fact, reached only Oklahoma when the thirty-day requirement ran out. But with the Armour Company's backing and his own pertinacity, Rodgers continued on from Oklahoma to Fort Worth and El Paso (he made twenty-three stops in Texas alone), then west to Tucson, and on to Pasadena, where 20,000 well-wishers

celebrated his successful completion of the first trans-continental flight by draping him in an American flag even though the crossing had taken him forty-nine days. The in-flight time for Rodgers was 82 hours and 2 minutes at an average speed of 52 mph. It beat driving; in 1903 when the first automobile traversed the United States it had taken sixty-five days. Four months after Rodgers reached Pasadena he was dead; during an exhibition flight he had crashed into the Pacific.

Wide World Photos

The Wright EX Vin Fiz *in which in 1911 cigar-smoking, ex-motorcycle racer Calbraith Perry Rodgers crashed nineteen times, made 69 stops, and lost the Hearst $50,000 prize en route to completing the first trans-continental flight across the United States.*

The huge high-wing monoplane that dominates the Pioneers of Flight gallery is the Fokker T-2 in which United States Army Lieutenants Oakley G. Kelly and John A. Macready took off from Long Island's Roosevelt Field on May 2, 1923, and not quite twenty-seven hours later landed at Rockwell Field in San Diego, California, thus completing the first successful U. S. *non-stop* coast-to-coast flight.

Kelly piloted the plane on takeoff and Macready was given the honor of landing.

The pilots exchanged places five times during the flight—an extraordinary maneuver which required that one man fly the plane from the near-blind rear controls within the fuselage (there was vision only to the sides) while the other abandoned the open cockpit, folded down the back of his seat, then opened a small triangular panel, then slithered through the opening and on back. The pilot in the rear would then snake his way forward to the open cockpit and once he was seated in the cold and drizzle he

In this giant Fokker T-2, Army Lieutenants Kelly and Macready completed the first successful non-stop U.S. coast-to-coast flight in 1923.

would shake the wheel to show he could now take over command. The Fokker T-2's first two attempts to cross the country had started in the west but because of the weight of the fuel-laden aircraft they could not gain enough altitude to climb over the mountains. The third and successful attempt was made by flying west from a take-off in the east. Here Lieutenant Macready discusses the successful flight:

We took off from Long Island at about 11:30 in the morning. It took us about a mile, maybe a mile and a half, to get off, and our wheels were still on the ground when we came to the drop-off from Roosevelt Field to Mitchell Field. We went over the ledge and down. Kelly was taking it off and I was behind. I was wondering, "Is it going to touch the ground? If it does, it's no use." But it maintained its flight and we just got over the hangars ahead. We had to keep from stalling and get just as much climb out of it as we could. Then we were over the water, near Staten Island, getting up around one hundred feet, maybe even a little more than that.

We got across the Alleghenies all right, but it began to get dark around Dayton, and it began to drizzle. You couldn't see anything but the lights of the cars on the highways, and we could only keep our compass from getting entirely out of control by checking it with the highways . . . . As long as you can see some outside fixed point you can balance your plane and everything's o.k. But if you've got nothing, you can't tell if you're upside down or how you are. I was flying then and there'd be times when you wouldn't get any outside point at all in the drizzle. We were over the Ozarks and I knew that if that kept up, I was just going to lose control of that plane. Then there'd be a light, some mountain cabin. Then you'd find you're cocked up on the side, but you're still going ahead. When you see that light, you can get yourself adjusted again . . . .

The impression that you get when you're flying across and you see no lights is that you're alone, and of course, we didn't know exactly where we were . . . . When we got out into Arizona the mountains were getting higher. We couldn't get over them so we had to deflect our course. We were just going over treetops, not very high, I'd say one hundred feet, something like that. Then we saw a place . . . a break in the mountains, and we came

through . . . and then pretty soon I saw a little town. You can work out a pattern by the way the railroads come in. Then you check it with your map. The town was nothing, but we were located. For the first time during the night we were located, the first time since St. Louis.

Then we were over Tehachapis and then down over San Diego. Well, as I said, we had the impression that nobody was interested. Then we came gliding toward North Island, and we came pretty close over the U. S. Grant Hotel. We saw a bunch of people on top of the hotel waving sheets and so forth. We went on and landed at Rockwell Field, and, of course, we were pretty tired when we got there.
—Oral History Collection of Columbia University

Nestled under the giant T-2's wing is another significant Army plane, a Douglas World Cruiser, one of two that completed the first successful around-the-world flight. By 1923 several long-range and endurance flights had succeeded and the goal of achieving an around-the-world flight was inevitable. The British had failed in 1922 and again in 1924. The Italians had failed then, too. But then on April 6, 1924, some of the United States Air Services' best pilots took off in four Douglas World Cruisers (modified Douglas DT torpedo planes) and on September 28, five months and 27,553 miles later, two of the planes completed the circle and returned once more to Seattle.

The flight's route spanned major oceans— the Pacific for the first time—and encountered weather extremes ranging from arctic to tropical. Although much of the support and safety facilities were provided by the United States Navy and the Coast Guard, conditions were often primitive. Fuel was rowed out to the World Cruisers in 55-gallon drums and had to be hand-pumped into the aircraft. The Douglas World Cruiser #1, the *Seattle*, piloted by Major Frederick L. Martin with Sergeant Alva Harvey as crew flew into heavy fog and low ceilings after taking off from Kanatak, Alaska, and struck a mountain slope and crashed. The men fortunately were not seriously injured and their ten-day "walk-out" to civilization is a story almost as remarkable as the flight itself. The Douglas World Cruiser #3, *Boston*, was lost en route to Iceland when engine trouble necessitated a forced landing in the ocean. Although its crew was rescued, the aircraft had to be abandoned in the rough seas.

Lieutenant Leslie P. Arnold, one of the four pilots successfully completing the circumnavigation of the globe, recalls the experience:

> The local papers intimated that there was not much hope that we would complete the journey, but as we circled over Seattle, I thought that there was at least a fifty-fifty chance . . . . The airplane was a biplane and had a metal framework covered with linen; there was a single Liberty engine of 400 horsepower. The maximum ceiling was around 8,000 feet so we had to fly under things instead of over them. There was just a small glass windshield in front of us, probably six inches high and eighteen inches in width. It was no protection at all unless you got way up under. It was nothing to have your shoulders wet through. They got iced up in no time at all.
>
> Nobody ever touched the planes save us. If an engine had to be changed, we changed it. We washed them, babied them, put them to bed. We did everything but sleep with them. After a flight we had a routine procedure which we followed. If the water connection had to be taped or shellacked, we did that—so we knew it wasn't going to fall down on the next hop. Everybody was a mechanic and everybody was a flier.
>
> . . . We had a forced landing in the jungles of Indochina. We were flying down the coast when a spray of water hit us. We knew that something had gone wrong in the engine. It began to heat up too much. We landed in the mouth of a river to discover that one of the cylinders had cracked. The other boys landed alongside. We had to get a new engine, so they took off and went to Tourane; Lowell Smith and I stayed in the airplane, sleeping on the wings. Finally, out of the darkness, came a Swedish voice. It was Erik Nelson [another one of the fliers]. He had made arrangements through Standard Oil and the local tribes, and we were towed up the river to the capital of the French kingdom of Annam. It was an interesting ride, with the natives in their sampans towing us. The chief was riding in his sampan with a parasol and with his favorite wives fanning him.
>
> The trip from Iceland to Greenland was the most frightening. We were two planes by that time. Everything was fine for about one hundred miles when we ran into fog and drizzle. We kept circling lower and lower until we were just over the water. There we saw broken ice and drifting icebergs, but we were past the point of no return and we had to keep going. So we plowed through this. The icebergs and the fog are both a dirty gray color, and it was very difficult flying seventy-five or one hundred feet off the water. We would veer here and there; when you saw one ahead there was no way to go except up in the fog. Finally we turned to the west and found the shore of Greenland. Then we had one hundred miles of clear weather and again ran into fog. We decided to stay on top this time, and kept our position by the mountain peaks. At last we arrived at a certain peak and thought the harbor should be under us. So we came down through the fog and landed in a nice little harbor. The second plane had not come in, however, and we went about our routine maintenance work, never saying a word. We felt too badly to say anything. But after about half an hour we heard the unmistakable noise of a Liberty engine. Then we had one of the finest parties Greenland had ever seen.
>
> Flying on from Greenland to Labrador, we got halfway across when two of our four gas pumps failed—we had to pump the gas by hand. It got tiresome and my arm began to get numb. So I thought the only way to do it was to use a combination of my belt and a handkerchief around my neck like a sling and to pull it with my other hand. I did that for close to four hours. It was tiresome, but it beat the hell out of swimming.
>
> —Oral History Collection of Columbia University

Certainly one of the most beautiful planes in the Air and Space Museum's collection is the little black-fuselaged biplane with floats that hangs suspended near the back wall and the *Vin Fiz*. It is the Curtiss R3C-2, flown on October 25, 1925, by United States Army Lieutenant James H. Doolittle in the course of winning the Schneider Trophy Race (limited to seaplanes) at a speed of 232.57 mph. The following day Doolittle set

A Douglas World Cruiser which in 1924 successfully completed the first round-the-world flight. Four of these modified torpedo planes took off from Seattle on April 6, 1924— five months and 27,553 miles later two of them safely returned.

In this handsome, sporty Curtiss R3C-2, U.S. Army Lieutenant Jimmy Doolittle won the 1925 Schneider Trophy Race (limited to seaplanes) with a speed of 232.57 mph.

a world speed record over a straight course with the same plane at a top speed of 245.7 mph. As the Curtiss R3C-1 with a fixed wheeled landing gear, the racer had won the Pulitzer Race earlier that same year. The R3C-2 was the last biplane to win the Schneider Trophy.

The other float plane in this gallery is the John K. Northrop-inspired Lockheed Sirius in which Charles A. Lindbergh and his wife Anne Morrow Lindbergh made two major flights in 1931 and 1933 to survey possible overseas airline routes in the early days of international air travel. The Lindberghs' 1931 "North-to-the-Orient" flight—the first east-to-west flight by way of the north—took them from Maine across Canada to Alaska and Siberia, over the Kurile Islands to Tokyo and finally to Lotus Lake near Nanking,

China, and demonstrated the feasibility of using the "Great Circle" route to reach the Far East.

Charles A. Lindbergh had described the flight as one with "no start or finish, no diplomatic or commercial significance, and no records to be sought"; but for the first half of their journey the Lindberghs flew where no airplane had flown before. The Sirius was equipped with Edo pontoons since the majority of their trip would be over water, and they wore electrically heated flying suits against the arctic cold. As one might anticipate of any journey across the ice packs to the Seward Peninsula, the frozen Bering Straits to Siberia and down to Japan, the Lindberghs encountered terrible weather and flying conditions. Anne Lindbergh was the radio operator and navigator. She was

During a stop in Greenland, the Lindberghs' Lockheed Sirius was christened Tingmissartoq ("the man who flies like a big bird") by an Eskimo boy.

responsible for keeping the outside world in touch with their progress, and it was often very trying for her to locate a radio station, tap out a Morse Code message and acknowledge the reply before she would have to haul in the antenna because her husband had found a hole in the clouds and could get low enough to confirm a reference point. Anne Lindbergh reported that the greatest compliment she had received on this flight was from another radio operator who had congratulated her on her skill in sending and receiving messages, saying, "No man could have done better."

The Lindberghs were offered the hospitality of the British aircraft carrier *Hermes,* which was anchored in the Yangtze River off Shanghai. At night the Sirius would be lifted out of the swollen river's

raging current. But, putting the Sirius back in the water one morning, the current caught the aircraft. Both Lindberghs were in the cockpits and as the current swung the plane, tipping it, the crane's cable caught against the Sirius' wing and their plane began to roll under. Lindbergh yelled to his wife to jump. He waited just long enough to see that she had surfaced safely, then he jumped into the river too. They were rescued by a tender, but the Sirius was too damaged to continue its flight and had to be returned to the United States for repairs.

Charles and Anne Lindbergh's next journey in the Sirius, which had been overhauled and refitted with a larger engine, was in 1933. Lindbergh was serving then as a technical advisor for Pan American Airways. With Anne Lindbergh again working as the navigator and radio operator, they took off from New York in July and flew up the eastern coast of Canada to Labrador,

In 1932, with this Lockheed Vega, Amelia Earhart made the first solo flight by a woman across the Atlantic.

then 650 miles across the water to Greenland. While there, a young Eskimo boy painted the word "Tingmissartoq" (meaning "the man who flies like a bird") on the Sirius' fuselage. From Greenland the Lindberghs flew their newly christened plane to Baffin Island and back before going on to Iceland. From Iceland, the Lindberghs flew to the major cities of Europe as far east as Moscow, then down the west coast of Africa, where they crossed the South Atlantic and flew down the Amazon River before turning north through the Caribbean and on back to the United States, where on December 19, they landed in New York. They had traveled some 30,000 miles across four continents, visited twenty-one countries, and gained invaluable information toward the planning of north and south Atlantic commercial airline routes.

That beautiful bright red Lockheed Vega— another John K. Northrop design—was used by Amelia Earhart during two historic flights in 1932: the first solo flight by a woman across the Atlantic, and the first solo flight by a woman across the United States. In 1935 she flew a similar Vega to become the first person—man *or* woman—to fly solo from Hawaii to the mainland of the United States.

Amelia Earhart had become interested in aviation in 1918 when she witnessed an exhibition of stunt flying while serving as a Red Cross nurse's aide in Canada. In June, 1928, she had become internationally famous overnight when she was the first woman to fly across the Atlantic, but she had been only a passenger and suffered the frustration of never once during the 20 hour and 40 minute flight being permitted to touch the controls. Although the world lavishly praised her courage in having made this flight, Amelia Earhart pointed out, "The bravest thing I did was to try to drop a bag of oranges and a note on the head of an ocean liner's captain—and I missed the whole ship." Determined to prove she could make the Atlantic crossing by herself, Amelia Earhart took off on May 20, 1932, from

Harbor Grace, Newfoundland, and immediately ran into bad weather. Ice accumulated on her bright red Vega's wings and at one point the weight of the ice forced her into a 3,000-foot uncontrollable descent. She did finally manage to level out when the warmer air near the ocean's surface cleared the ice, but it wasn't until 14 hours and 52 minutes of having fought heavy storms and terrible fatigue that she landed in a field in Northern Ireland, 2,026 miles from her starting point. She was, of course, celebrated upon her return but instead of basking in admiration she prepared for her second flight, the first woman's solo non-stop transcontinental hop.

Amelia Earhart, in the same Vega, took off from Los Angeles, on August 24, and 19 hours and 5 minutes later landed in Newark having covered the 2,448-mile distance at an average speed of 128½ mph. The Vega was the first airplane built by the Lockheed Aircraft Company and established its tradition for excellence in design.

In 1937, Amelia Earhart and her navigator Fred Noonan lost their lives while attempting a round-the-world flight in a twin-engined Lockheed Electra. Noonan and Miss Earhart had reached New Guinea in late June of that year and their next stop was to be Howland Island, a tiny dot 2,556 miles across the South Pacific. Noonan had reported having trouble setting his chronometers, time pieces whose accuracy is essential in determining longitudinal measurements during navigation over water. But ignoring Noonan's misgivings, Amelia Earhart and her navigator took off from New Guinea on July 2 and headed west. The *Itasca*, a United States Coast Guard vessel stationed at sea near Howland Island, received radio messages from Miss Earhart and Noonan reporting strong headwinds and heavy fuel consumption. A final fragmentary message was received indicating that the Electra was off course, lost. Then no further messages were received and the radio was silent. No trace of the aircraft or its crew has ever been found.

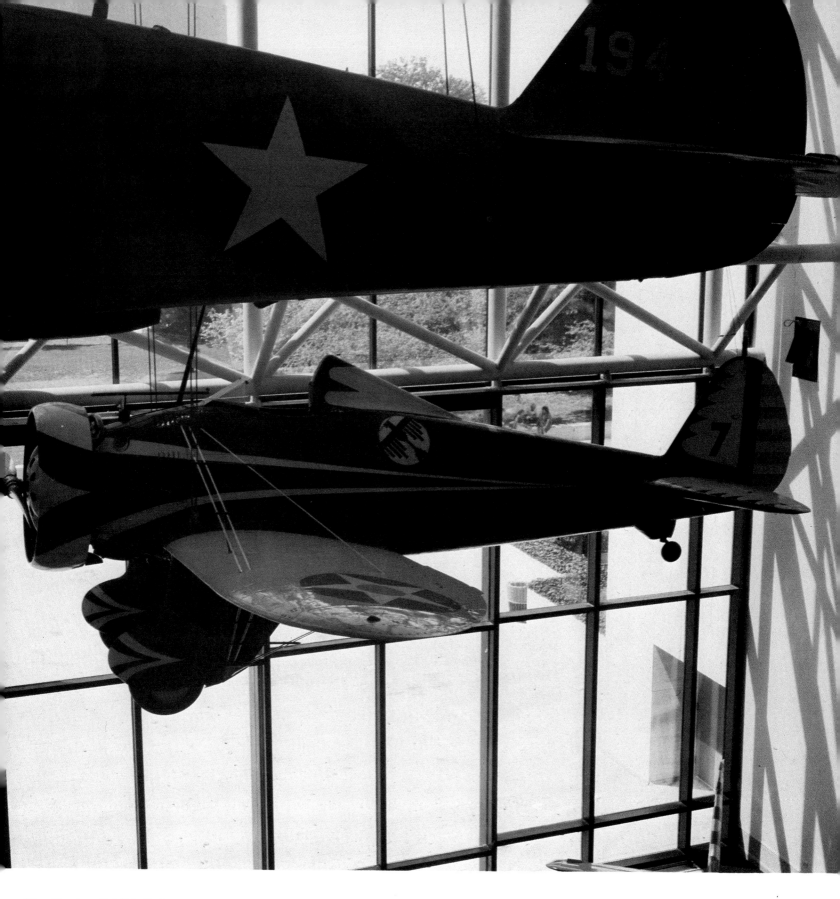

The Boeing P-26A fighter was America's first line of air defense in the mid- and late 1930s. Nicknamed the "Peashooter", the P-26 was the first all-metal American fighter and the last to have an open cockpit, fixed landing gear, and externally braced wings. After restoration at the Garber Facility, it now hangs in the West Gallery.

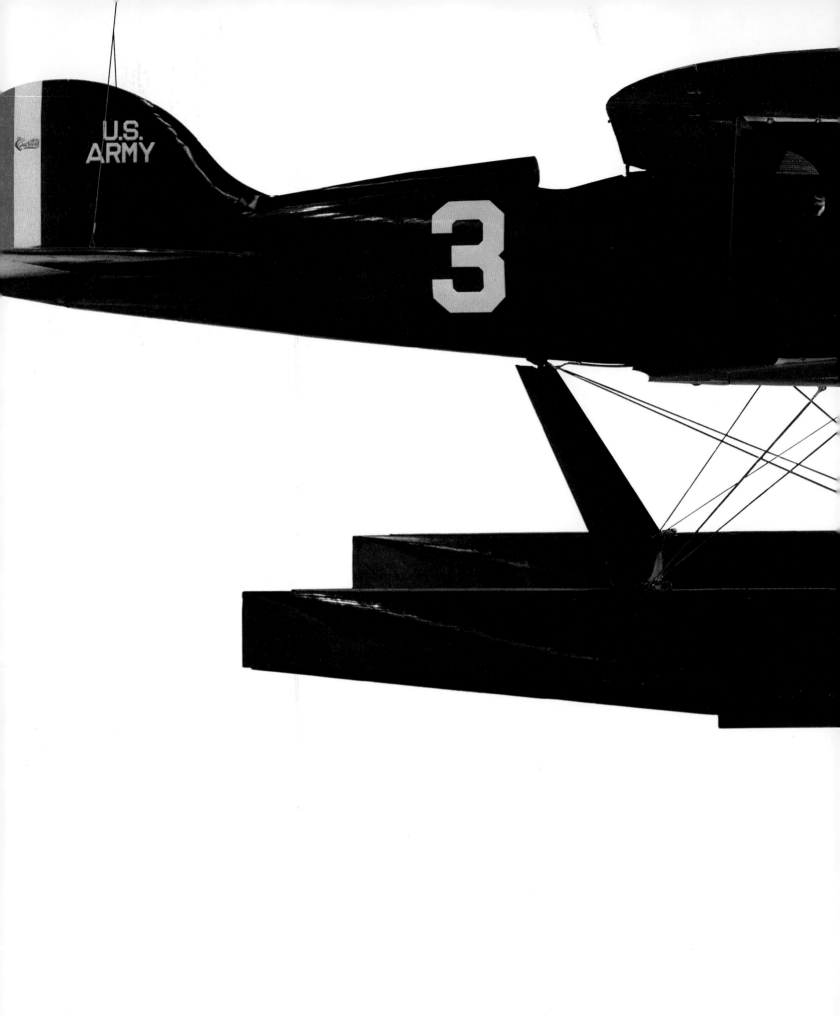

The great air races provided the major impetus to aviation during the 1920s. Jimmy Doolittle's Curtiss R3C-2 fitted with pontoons won the 1925 Schneider Trophy Race. Designated the R3C-1 and fitted with a fixed landing gear, this same plane, only two weeks earlier, had won the 1925 Pulitzer Race for landplanes.

One of the most colorful racing pilots of the 1930s was Roscoe Turner, who favored powder blue military-type uniforms and often flew with "Gilmore," a lion cub, as a companion. In the Turner RT-14 Meteor depicted here he won both the 1938 and 1939 Thompson Trophy Races.

One of the world's all-time great aerobatic aircraft, this Bücker 133 Jungmeister was airfreighted to this country on board the Hindenburg in 1936.

Hall of Air Transportation

Visitors to the National Air and Space Museum almost automatically turn from the Milestones of Flight gallery to the Hall of Air Transportation. Perhaps it is the irresistible attraction of seeing how something as huge as a DC-3—at 17,500 pounds, the heaviest aircraft supported by the Museum structure—can be hung from the ceiling as effortlessly as if it were nothing more than a young boy's model airplane suspended on a fishing leader.*

Each of the aircraft on display in this hall played a significant role in the development of air transportation, a field which commenced in this country only a little more than ten years after the Wright brothers' first powered flight, when A. C. Phiel, the former mayor of St. Petersburg, Florida, paid $400 for the privilege of becoming, on January 1, 1914, the St. Petersburg-Tampa Air Boat Line's first passenger. The airline's wooden-hulled Benoist Type XIV biplane flying boat made two eighteen-mile round-trip flights per day between Tampa and St. Petersburg, and the twenty-three-minute one-way trip began regularly scheduled airline service in the United States. The Benoist XIV's top speed was 63 mph, and when three months later the contract had ended, 1,204 passengers had paid $5.00 each for the one-way flight in the plane's open cockpit. The St. Petersburg-Tampa Air Boat Line lost only eight days due to weather or mechanical failure during its ninety days of operation and in addition to maintaining a regular schedule, the company pioneered some advanced airline concepts: excess baggage weight or passenger weight (any passenger weighing over 200 pounds) was charged at the rate of $5.00 per hundred pounds.

Commercial flying in this country, however, had floundered about until May 20, 1927, when Charles A. Lindbergh took off from New York City's Roosevelt Field. His landing 33 hours and 30 minutes later in Paris had an extraordinary impact on American aviation. It was as though some vast psychological barrier had been crossed. Within the following year the applications for private pilot's licenses jumped from 1,800 to 5,500. In 1928 the nation's still-fledgling airlines doubled their route-miles flown, tripled the amount of mail carried, and quadrupled the number of passengers. From the moment Lindbergh landed at Le Bourget outside of Paris people realized that the airplane had suddenly come of age: airplanes could actually span continents and oceans, cross over mountains and arctic wastes. They could deliver passengers, mail, and merchandise with what America loved most of all: speed. The key factor in explaining the sudden enormous expansion of American commercial flying is that big business had

---

*The answer lies in the genius of the Museum building's design: aircraft are hung from the triangular steel trusses that span the ceiling between the upright pylons. The trusses, which are triangular in cross section as well, provide enormous strength while creating a sense of openness and space. This technique, similar to that used to strengthen aircraft structure, makes it possible to suspend several loads along an entire span or to concentrate one major weight in one place.

come to realize that big money could be made—but only if commercial aviation were run on a businesslike basis. That meant mergers and subsidies.

In 1927 Juan Trippe had received the mail contract between Key West, Florida, and Cuba. In 1928 he won additional foreign mail contracts to the Canal Zone and Puerto Rico. This meant that his young Pan American Airways would be guaranteed a backing of at least two and a half million dollars a year in mail-contract revenues. By 1931 he had locked up South America and successfully prevented foreign airlines from dominating that continent. By this time, too, three major airline companies had emerged out of the tangle of competitive small carriers in the United States: United Airlines, American Airlines, and TWA.

In 1929 Transcontinental Air Transport (TAT)—which had become known as "The Lindbergh Line" when Lindbergh agreed to the use of his name—offered a unique transcontinental service requiring their passengers to split the trip between Ford Tri-Motors and Pullman-car trains. The Fords flew only in daylight across the safe flying country; the passengers would then board the train for the nighttime passage over the mountains. Although the trip could be made in relative safety, it was not a commercial success since the 48-hour journey across the country was not all that competitive with the railroads alone. The next year TAT merged with Western Air Express and became Transcontinental and Western Air, or TWA.

That same year United Airlines, which flew the Chicago and West Coast route, bought National Air Transport, whose routes were between Chicago and New York. In the south a gaggle of small carriers combined to become American Airlines.

In March, 1929, these three big systems came under the penetrating eye of Walter F. Brown, Postmaster General of the new Hoover Administration. Like his predecessors, Brown felt that the Post Office Department should encourage commercial aviation in the interests of national defense. But he also felt that rapid expansion would never take place so long as government subsidies made it more profitable for the airlines to carry mail than to carry passengers.

Consequently, he sought an amendment to the original Kelly Act that would eliminate the old pound-per-mile rate and pay operators according to how much cargo space they made available. Brown figured that this would encourage the airlines to place orders for larger airplanes; then, if mail did not fill the extra space, the operator would carry passengers rather than fly half-empty. The new proposal, passed as the McNary-Watres Bill, also attempted to reward progressive operators by providing for extra payments to airlines using multi-engine planes equipped with the latest navigational aids. The whole point of the new law, Brown said, was to develop aviation in the broad sense and to stimulate manufacturers "who would compete with each other and bring their aeronautical industry up to the point where it could finally sustain itself."

This approach meant, inevitably, that when it came to bestowing mail contracts Brown would tend to disregard the small, struggling, independent airlines in favor of the larger companies with better financing and more experienced personnel. After a series of meetings, later known sardonically as the "Spoils Conference," the big operators did walk off with most of the contracts.

—*The American Heritage History of Flight*, by Arthur Gordon

United Airlines won the northern transcontinental route, TWA the central route, and American Airlines the southern. The size of the country, itself, had become a factor advantageous to the growth of air travel. Aircraft companies competed with each other to come up with the fastest, safest, and most economical planes. And it is this competition that resulted in some of the revolutionary designs one sees in the aircraft exhibited in this hall.

Let's begin on the floor of the Hall of Air Transportation with the rotating beacon light next to the Douglas M-2 mailplane with the Western Airlines markings. Before sophisticated radio navigation rendered beacon lights obsolete, pilots relied upon lights such as the one exhibited that were spaced approximately ten miles apart along the routes flown between major cities. In

A 1920s Douglas M-2 mailplane beneath a rotating beacon navigation aid.

*The Museum's Pitcairn Mailwing
in Eastern Air Transport markings.*

1946 there were 2,112 airways beacons on 124 air routes in the United States. At night under fair weather conditions a pilot could see one or more of these lights at any given time. Pilots learned the following mnemonic to help them remember the code flashed by the various airways beacon lights: **W**(.--)hen **U**(..-)ndertaking **V**(...-)ery **H**(....)ard **R**(.-.)outes **K**(-.-)eep **D**(-..)irections **B**(-...)y **G**(--.)ood **M**(--)ethods. Starting at the origin of the airway, the successive rotating beacon lights would flash the International Morse Code for the letters **W, U, V, H, R, K, D, B, G,** and **M**; this sequence would start again with the eleventh and twenty-first light, etc. The beacon on exhibit in the Museum once stood on a 60-foot-high tower on White Water Hill in California; it blinks two long and one short flash, the code letter "**G**," indicating it was the ninth beacon from the origin of the airway, Los Angeles.

The Douglas M-2 mailplane exhibited next to the beacon was one of a family of large biplanes built between the mid- and late-1920s by the Douglas Aircraft Company as a replacement for the venerable DH-4s used previously to fly the mails. The M-2 was a fast, sturdy, dependable aircraft. The Museum's Douglas M-2 was originally delivered to the Post Office Department in 1926; Western Air Express acquired it in 1927 and flew the plane approximately 914 hours before it crashed on January 23, 1930. The plane was sold and, after passing through several owners' hands, was repurchased by Western Air Express' successor, Western Airlines, in 1940. The M-2 was restored to flying condition in 1976 in time to celebrate Western Airlines' Fiftieth Anniversary, which was the record for the longest continuous airline service in the United States.

Above the Douglas M-2 hangs the sporty Pitcairn PA-5 Mailwing, which was designed specifically for the shorter mail routes in the eastern United States. The aircraft's efficiency and economical operating costs stemmed from three factors: a clean, lightweight airframe (utilizing wooden wings and easily fabricated square tubing in the fuselage—both fabric covered), the remarkably reliable Wright Whirlwind engine (the same type of engine used by Lindbergh's *Spirit of St. Louis*), and the Pitcairn-designed airfoil and pronounced dihedral in the lower wing which permitted a relatively high speed, stability, and load-carrying capability.

The Mailwing's reputation was established on the New York-to-Atlanta mail-contract run flown by the Pitcairn Aircraft Company starting May 1, 1928, where by following the newly lighted airways between New York, Philadelphia, Baltimore, Washington, Richmond, and Atlanta the little Pitcairn Mailwings were able to make the 760-mile journey at night in seven hours—one-third the length of time it took by train. On December 1, 1928, Pitcairn Aircraft took over the Atlanta-Miami mail route, thereby creating the basic airline route upon which its successor, Eastern Air Transport (later Eastern Airlines), would establish so successful a service. The Museum's Mailwing survived both a crash and use as a crop duster before being repurchased by Eastern Airlines employees, who restored it and presented it to Captain Edward V. Rickenbacker, who was the Eastern Airlines Company's president for so many years.

The silver monoplane with the TWA markings hanging between the Pitcairn Mailwing and the Fairchild FC-2 is the Northrop Alpha, one of the most beautiful airplanes in the Museum's collection. Designed by the legendary John K. "Jack" Northrop (who also designed Amelia Earhart's Lockheed Vega in the Pioneers of Flight gallery), the Alpha represents a transition in air transport design. Four passengers were enclosed in the snug, comfortable heated cabin while the pilot sat above and behind them in the open cockpit exposed to the elements in the traditional mailplane manner. The Alpha's advanced all-metal design included the Northrop multicellular cantilevel wing, a semi-monocoque fuselage, and streamlined N.A.C.A. cowling. The shaped fairings

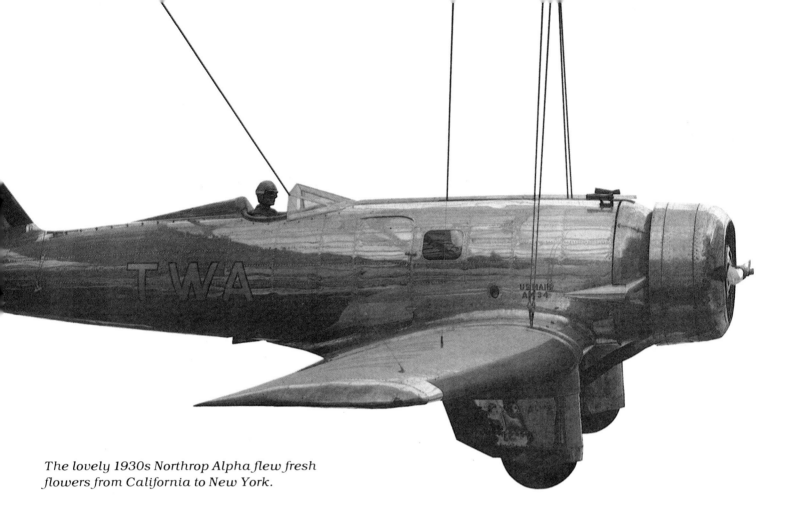

The lovely 1930s Northrop Alpha flew fresh flowers from California to New York.

around the fixed landing gear provided drag reduction without the weight and complexity of a retractable undercarriage. Introduced in 1930, the Alpha was designed to be a swift, dependable airplane that could carry passengers and freight out of small airfields. With the coming of the newer, larger twin-engined Boeing and Douglas transports in 1933 and 1934, the Northrop Alphas were soon relegated to freight-carrying roles in which they flew coast-to-coast in 23 hours, bringing from California such exotic commodities as fresh-cut gardenias, silkworms, and serums to New York. Although the Alpha was in use for only a few years, its major importance lay in the advanced design concepts engineered by Northrop which were of fundamental importance in the construction of the Douglas DC-2 and DC-3.

Perhaps no aircraft has been the subject of more legends, admiration, and misconceptions than the Ford Tri-Motor, one of which hangs just in front of the DC-3. Affectionately known as the "Tin Goose," the Ford Tri-Motor was the largest civil aircraft in America when it started passenger service on August 2, 1926.

The Tri-Motor's all-metal construction, the implied massive strength of its thick wings, the prestige of the Ford name, all combined with the pure lucky timing of its debut. This happily coincided with the worldwide love affair with aviation resulting from Lindbergh's same year New York-to-Paris flight and made the Ford Tri-Motor an immediate success with the public.

Inertial starters activated the Ford's three engines. A mechanic or the co-pilot would insert a crank in each engine and, on signal, begin cranking. Slowly at first the heavy flywheel geared to the engine's crankshaft would turn and then as the speed increased and the flywheel began to whine at what sounded like full speed,

the cranker pulled a cable which engaged a spring-loaded clutch thereby transmitting the energy of the spinning wheel to turn the engine. The squealing sound was almost identical to that displeasure emitted by a

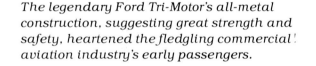

The legendary Ford Tri-Motor's all-metal construction, suggesting great strength and safety, heartened the fledgling commercial aviation industry's early passengers.

resentful pig kicked in anger. If the oil was not too cold the propeller would turn at least three or four revolutions. Usually this was enough to start the engine, but if the pilot was not alert and missed the moment of truth with mixture and throttle, the crankee was obliged to start his labors all over again. Winding the cranks was very hard work and at times when the engines proved unaccountably balky there were impolite exchanges of opinion between cockpit and cranker.

. . . life with and aboard the tri-motored Fords was far from ideal . . . . Ford passenger cabins were always too hot or too cold and decibel level assured them a top place among the world's noisiest aircraft. Immediately on boarding, passengers were offered chewing gum which would allegedly ease the pressure changes on their eardrums during climb and descent, but it was just as much to encourage a cud-chewing state of nerves. They were also offered cotton which wise passengers stuffed in

their ears so they would be able to hear ordinary conversation once they were again on the ground . . . .

In the first Fords there were no seat belts. Only hand grips were provided to stabilize passengers, and summertime flying could become a purgatory. While they bounced around in low-altitude turbulence the passengers muttered about "air pockets" and a high percentage became airsick. Even with a few windows open the cabin atmosphere developed a sourness which only time and scrubbing could remove.

If the passengers retreated to the lavatory they found little comfort at any season. In winter the expedition became a trial-by-refrigeration since the toilet consisted of an ordinary seat with cover. Once the cover was raised for whatever purpose there was revealed a bombardier's direct view of the passing landscape several thousand feet below, and the chill factor in the compartment instantly discouraged any loitering.

Even in smooth air flying a Ford became a chore if only because it was so difficult to keep in trim. The man who could coax a Ford into flying hands-off for even a few minutes was temporarily in luck and probably did not have any passengers. Even a normal bank in a Ford was an experiment in muscular coordination mixed with a practiced eye for anticipation since whatever physical input was directed to the controls a relatively long time passed before anything happened. To stop or reverse as desired *any* maneuver required a keen sense of anticipatory delay. In rough air these delays and willfulness were compounded, and just keeping the Ford straight and level became a workout. In a thunderstorm or line squall the pilots sometimes wondered who was in charge of affairs.

In the devious way of legends the Ford has somehow emerged as a stable aircraft. In the sense that they were always controllable and therefore safe the recognition is true, but no more is deserved. Legend also has it that Fords could be landed in any small cow pasture, which was not so, particularly if loaded. The ability lies somewhere in between, depending on many factors, including the hunger status of the pilot or airline. Takeoff performance was actually more remarkable than landing speeds, which were much higher than most historians seem inclined to acknowledge. Perhaps they do not realize that behind the more spectacular short-field stops made by Fords which actually touched down between 65 and 70 miles per hour, there was a grunting copilot pulling for all he was worth on the long [Johnson] bar which extended from the floor upward between the two cockpit seats. The bar activated the hydraulic brakes which in their own obstinate way gave airline mechanics perpetual trouble.

—*Ernest K. Gann's Flying Circus*, by Ernest K. Gann

When United Airlines' huge order for these 247Ds monopolized Boeing's production lines, competing airlines were forced to turn to other aircraft companies. Douglas' response—the DC-1—was a design that rendered Boeing's airplane immediately obsolete.

Ford Tri-Motor passengers sat on wicker seats chosen for their strength, lightness, and comfort. The first models of this plane carried twelve passengers, later models as many as fourteen at 110 mph. The most distinctive aspect of the aircraft was its rugged all-metal construction readily identified by its corrugated aluminum skin. Its only rival was the tri-motored Fokker to whose design the Ford owed so much. But when one of these Fokkers crashed, killing Notre Dame's famous football coach, Knute

Rockne, and blame for the crash was placed on the structural failure of the Fokker's wooden construction, the Ford Tri-Motor emerged as the unchallenged transport of that era.

The Boeing 247D, the first truly modern airliner, was a pioneer whose clean lines readily distinguished it from the tri-motors and biplanes it had immediately rendered obsolete. When it entered service in 1933 its design features included low-wing all-metal construction necessitating a padded step in

the middle of the passenger aisle beneath which the main wing spar was located. This inconvenience was accepted as a visible proof of the great structural strength of the plane. Its retractable landing gear was clean and simple; the wheels protruded slightly, thereby providing some protection should a wheels-up landing be necessary. And its 550 hp Pratt and Whitney Wasp engines were supercharged to provide a top speed of 200 mph in later models.

In 1937 United Air Lines ordered sixty 247s, thereby fully tying up Boeing's production lines and effectively denying the use of that plane by any other airline. On May 22, 1933, when the new Boeing 247D went into service on the cross-country run, it made the flight from San Francisco to New York in 19½ hours—knocking eight and a half hours off the previous 27-hour flying time. The original 247 had a cruising speed of 170 mph compared to the 110 mph speed of the Ford Tri-Motor then in general use. The tactic of preventing other airlines from

purchasing the Boeing 247 worked to a disadvantage for United Air Lines since it forced TWA to go to Douglas for an aircraft that could compete.

Between the Ford Tri-Motor and the Boeing 247 hangs the Douglas DC-3, the single most important aircraft in the history of air transportation. Almost every Museum visitor is familiar with it; many have flown in it as a commercial airliner or in its military C-47 version. Until 1934, airline passenger planes were either too slow or carried too few passengers to create much profit. The Boeing 247 carried only ten passengers and it was at about this time that airline companies could no longer depend upon airmail contracts for their primary source of income. When Transcontinental and Western Airways (to become TWA) ordered Douglas to develop an airplane capable of competing with the Boeing monopolized by United Air Lines, Douglas came up with the DC-1. On its maiden flight, July 1, 1933, the DC-1

exceeded all of TWA's specifications. Only one DC-1 was built. On May 18, 1934, the first production DC-2 went into service with TWA on the Columbus-Newark route. It could carry fourteen passengers in comfort and it was fast. The DC-2 began its career by breaking the commercial New York-to-Chicago speed record four times in eight days. So many airlines ordered the DC-2 that Douglas had to carefully schedule deliveries. The beginnings of the "Great Silver Fleet" came when Eastern Air Lines ordered fourteen DC-2s for its New York-Miami route. Although the DC-2 resembled the Boeing 247 in some ways, it offered major advantages: the overall design was aerodynamically cleaner, it used the more powerful Wright R-1820 engines (875 hp), had split-trailing edge flaps, and controllable pitch propellers. The DC-3 came about when C. R. Smith, the President of American Airlines, asked Douglas to build a larger version of the DC-2 that could be fitted with

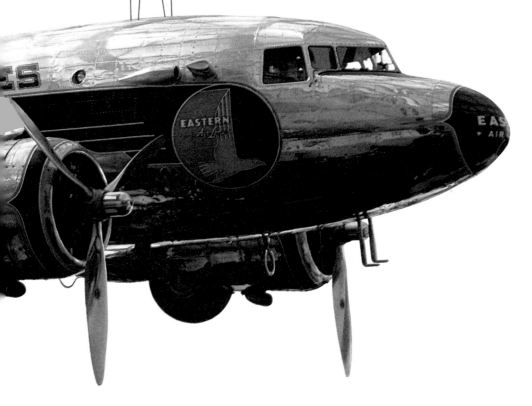

The Douglas DC-3, the single most important aircraft in the history of air transportation—and the heaviest airplane suspended in the Museum.

fourteen berths so that passengers could sleep on the long transcontinental flights. This version became the Douglas Sleeper Transport, the DST. The DST was not a financial success and was turned into the DC-3, which was identical except that instead of sleeping berths the aircraft was fitted with twenty-one seats.

The DC-3's success was due to the fact that it was the first airplane in the world that could make money by hauling passengers only. The flying public liked the plane. Its 180 mph cruising speed was the fastest of its day, and it carried eleven passengers more than the Boeing 247 and in greater comfort. It was considered much safer than any previous transport. Pilots liked its stability, ease of handling, and single-engine performance. The airlines liked it because it was reliable and inexpensive to operate. By 1938, 80 percent of all American commercial airline traffic was carried on DC-3s. And by the next year most of all the airline traffic in

the world was carried on DC-3s.

The DC-3 displayed in the Hall of Air Transportation made its last commercial flight on October 12, 1952, when it flew from San Salvador to Miami. By then it had flown more than 56,700 hours! The DC-3 has proved itself the most popular transport airplane ever built.

Even though the engineering of the DC-3 was advanced for its day, uncertainties on the part of its designers led to the aircraft's being built much stronger than necessary. Much of its strength came from the multicellular stressed-wing construction devised by Jack Northrop, a technique employing many small formed-metal members rather than the until-then traditional rib-and-spar wing design. The redundancy of its strength made it possible for the DC-3 to operate under difficult conditions. During the war the military version of the DC-3, the C-47, was used by the thousands in every theater of the war.

Affectionately nicknamed "Gooney Bird," they were flown over the Hump, over Europe, and in the Pacific. After the war, many of the surplus C-47s were converted back into civilian transports. Almost every warring power used the DC-3 or a license-built derivative. The Russians used C-47s supplied by Lend-Lease and Lisunov LI-2s made in Russia; the Japanese built a series known as an L2D. Because post-war surplus made it possible to purchase a C-47 at a low price, innumerable small airlines were created with but one or two of these converted aircraft. Over 9,123 C-47s were built during the war, and there is probably not a nation in the world today where one cannot find at least one DC-3 still flying.

On the floor of the hall rests a smaller twin-engine Beechcraft Model 18—an airplane that was first produced on January 15, 1937, and remained in production for almost thirty-three years, the longest production span of any aircraft in history. It was designed as a rugged, fast, easily maintained aircraft and was used by a large number of smaller airlines. Its greatest

impact on general aviation lay in its use for many years as the most prestigious of the executive transports. During most of its more than thirty-two-year production it was considered the best small twin-engine transport in the world.

The ultimate development in large piston-engine airliners was the Douglas DC-7. American Airlines introduced this model on its New York-to-Los Angeles run on November 29, 1953, and it became the first airliner to offer non-stop service from either coast. The DC-7 cruised at 360 mph and was the fastest aircraft in service; as a result, eighteen different airlines ordered these planes. The nose section of the DC-7 displayed in the Museum is from the American Airlines flagship *Vermont*, which carried about 130,000 passengers in its almost 13,500 hours aloft. With the advent of the faster, turbine-engine powered Boeing 707s, the piston-engine airliner became obsolete.

Should the Museum visitor wonder why the NASM does not exhibit a Boeing 747 "Jumbo Jet," the answer is simple: the aircraft is so huge, it wouldn't fit.

Balloons and Airships

Everybody *knows* hot air rises; still, visitors to the Balloons and Airships gallery seem momentarily stunned to *see* the principle in action right at the entrance, but soon they become drawn by one of the most colorful and striking exhibits in the gallery: the large facsimile of the Montgolfier balloon in which on November 21, 1783, one hundred and twenty years before the Wright brothers achieved powered flight at Kill Devil Hill, two daring Frenchmen, Pilâtre de Rozier and the Marquis d'Arlandes, made the first sustained aerial flight. The Montgolfier hot-air balloon in which this ascent was made was 70 feet high and 46 feet in diameter; the balloon's covering was blue cotton cloth embroidered in gold with lions' heads, eagles, anthropomorphized suns, the ornamental devices of that era, and signs of the zodiac. The hot air that made the 1,600-pound balloon lift was furnished by the heat rising from dry straw burned on an iron grate directly beneath the open neck of the huge balloon.

Ten days after Pilâtre de Rozier and the Marquis d'Arlandes' flight, Professor J. A. C. Charles made the first free ascension in a hydrogen balloon incorporating many of the essential features of modern balloons. Professor Charles and a companion—one of the Robert brothers who had earlier shown Charles how to construct a balloon capable of containing the hydrogen within its envelope through coating its silk covering with rubber—took off in an elaborately gilded wicker-work car suspended beneath their small candy-striped balloon from the Tuileries Gardens. Their balloon, equipped with food, extra clothing, scientific instruments, and ballast bags of sand, rose swiftly 800 feet into the air as Professor Charles and Monsieur Robert waved flags to the assembled crowds below. Professor Charles, who was able to control the ascent and descent of his balloon by dumping ballast and by opening a crude valve at the top of the balloon that permitted the hydrogen to escape, thus quickly proved the superiority of the gas or hydrogen-filled *Charlières* over the slow, fire-breathing, clumsy hot-air *Montgolfières*. In the two-hour flight the balloon was carried by the wind twenty-seven miles from Paris to Nesle where, at dusk, the two men brought themselves gently down to the ground. Monsieur Robert got out and Professor Charles decided to make one more ascent; the balloon lightened now by one less occupant, sprang up to 9,000 feet, and Charles became the first man to see the sun set twice in one day. But because of the cold and a sharp altitude-pressure pain in his ear, Professor Charles descended soon after.

The story is told that Benjamin Franklin, while visiting Paris that same year, witnessed one of the first balloon ascents. Many of those about him saw no practical value in the flights, and a French Army officer present with Mr. Franklin although impressed by the balloon's beauty and value as a toy asked, "But of what use is it?" Franklin, who was always quick to appreciate the potential significance of any new scientific experiment, is supposed to have replied, "Of what use is a new born baby?"

These first balloon adventures generated the most enormous excitement—an excitement which might be difficult for us to understand today; but if one strolls through the gallery and looks at some of the snuff boxes, prints, tapestries, inlaid furniture, cabinets, china and enamels all with ballooning motifs, it may help to understand that balloons were in their time a craze comparable, say, to the Beatles.

A puppet theater in this gallery reenacts the dramatic 1785 aerial crossing of the English Channel for the first time by two of the least convivial aeronauts in history: the French pilot Jean-Pierre Blanchard and his American-born patron and passenger Dr.

John Jeffries. Blanchard had become interested in flight in 1777 when he began experimenting with parachutes. In 1781 he built a "flying chariot," a man-powered ornithopter with four beating wings that, of course, did not fly. But with the success of the *Charlière* balloons he gave up heavier-than-air flight and concentrated his attention on ballooning and made several successful ascents. Dr. John Jeffries was so taken by Blanchard's triumphs that he was determined to make a flight with Blanchard across the English Channel—so determined, in fact, that as Jeffries later wrote in his *A Narrative of the Two Aerial Voyages of Dr. Jeffries*, published in London in 1786, "I agreed with M. Blanchard in consideration of my engaging to furniſh him with all the materials and labour to fill the Balloon; and to pay all the expenſes of tranſporting them to Dover." There, while waiting for more auspicious weather, Blanchard, who wanted the honor of making the first Channel crossing all to himself, made every effort to get rid of Jeffries. The quarrel was resolved only when the Governor of Dover Castle intervened and heard Dr. Jeffries explain how he had paid all of Blanchard's London debts thereby alone making it possible for Blanchard "*to purſue this* experiment," and that Jeffries had even agreed "in case of neceſſity on our paſſage, *I would get out* of the Car *for his preſervation.*" Furthermore, Jeffries explained to the Governor, he "was refolved to undertake the Voyage at all events, without M. Blanchard, unlefs he thought proper to accompany me, without further artifice or objection; as I was fully fatiffied of the practicability of the plan."

At one in the afternoon on January 7, 1785, Blanchard and Jeffries lifted off for the coast of France. With them in the car suspended beneath the balloon were "three ſacks of ſand ballaſt, of ten pounds each; a large parcel of pamphlets, two cork jackets, a few extra cloaths of M. Blanchard; a number of inflated bladders, with two ſmall anchors or grapnels, with cords affixed, to affift our landing." Attached to the car was a

moulinet—a hand-cranked propeller and some aerial oars. The balloon "roſe ſlowly and majeſtically" over the edge of the Dover cliff, then, as thousands watched, drifted slowly out to sea and "paſſed over ſeveral veſſels of different kinds, which ſaluted us with their colours, as we paſſed them; and we began to overlook and have an extenſive view of the coaſt of France; which enchanting views of England and France being alternately preſented to us by the rotary and ſemi-circular motion of the Balloon and Car greatly increaſed the beauty and variety of our ſituation."

When Blanchard and Jeffries had reached 2,000 feet thirty minutes into their voyage, the balloon had swollen to its utmost extent and it became necessary to vent some of the gas. Twenty minutes later it became obvious they had released too much for Jeffries "found we were deſcending faſt." They cast out one and a half sacks of ballast and the balloon steadied; but with two-thirds of the Channel still to cross, their balloon began to lose altitude again, and they "were obliged to caſt out the remaining ſack and an half of ballaſt, ſacks and all; notwithstanding which, not finding that we roſe, we caſt out a parcel of pamphlets, and in a minute or two found, that we roſe again."

At two-fifteen they had to throw overboard the remaining pamphlets. At two-thirty, Jeffries "found we were again deſcending very rapidly . . . . We immediately threw out all the little things we had with us, ſuch as biſcuits, apples, &c. and after that one of our oars or wings; but ſtill deſcending, we caſt away the other wing, and then the governail . . . and unſcrewing the moulinet, I likewiſe caſt that into the ſea . . . " The balloon continued to lose altitude so "we cut away all the lining and ornaments, both within and on the outſide of the Car and . . . threw them into the ſea." Overboard next went their only bottle of cognac, the anchors and cords; "but ſtill approaching the ſea, we began to *ſtrip ourſelves,* and caſt away our cloathing, M. Blanchard firſt throwing away his *extra coat* . . . after which I threw away my *only* coat;

and then M. Blanchard his other coat and trowfers: We then put on . . . our cork jackets, and prepared for the event," a crash landing into the sea.

At last, as they neared the coast of France, their balloon again began to rise—higher in fact than it had reached before and as a result "from the lofs of our cloaths, we were almoft benumbed with cold." The wind had increased and the two intrepid voyagers soon found themselves descending again and fast approaching a forest. Over land at last they cast away their cork life preservers but "we had now approached fo near to the tops of the trees of the foreft, as to difcover that they were very large and rough, and that we were defcending with great velocity towards them." There was nothing left for them to throw overboard and then it suddenly occurred to Jeffries "that probably we might be able to fupply it from within ourfelves, from the recollection that we had drunk much at breakfaft, and not having had any evacuation . . . that probably an extra quantity had been fecreted by the kidneys, which we might avail ourfelves by difcharging. I inftantly propofed my idea to M. Blanchard, and the event fully juftified my expectation; . . . however trivial or ludicrous it may feem, I have reafon to believe [the act] was of *real utility* to us, *in our then fituation*; for by cafting it away, as we were approaching fome trees of the foreft higher than the reft, it fo altered our courfe, that inftead of being forced hard againft, or into them, we paffed along near them . . . as enabled me to catch hold of the topmoft branches of one of them and thereby arreft the further progrefs of the Balloon." Branch by branch Jeffries and Blanchard guided the balloon to an open spot where they could let it sink to the ground. They landed with what must have been the most enormous relief about twelve miles inland from Calais and the open sea; and thus completed the first crossing of the English Channel by air. It would be almost 125 years before the Channel would be crossed by a heavier-than-air flying machine; a Frenchman would be at the controls then, too: Louis Blériot on July 25, 1909, crossed the twenty miles of open water in a monoplane of his own design in thirty-seven minutes.

Toward the end of the Nineteenth Century

A replica of the Hindenburg's *control cabin made for a motion picture about the* Hindenburg. *Passengers on the 804-foot-long* Hindenburg *paid $720 apiece for a round-trip ticket between the United States and Germany*

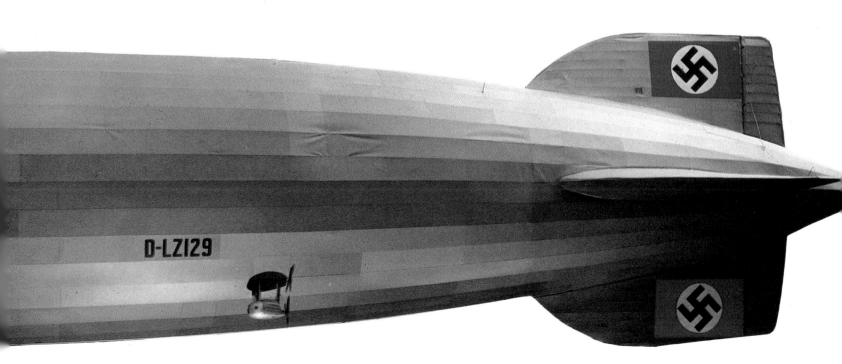

enough had been learned about structures, streamlining, power plants, and control devices to construct powered balloons or airships that could be flown successfully. But it wasn't until Count von Zeppelin of Germany—an avid balloonist who recognized the enormous reconnaissance potential of dirigibles as well as the structural and weight-carrying limitations of the blimps then being built—that a sensational breakthrough in dirigible design was achieved by creating motorized airships with a rigid construction. The lifting gas bags or balloons were contained within and fastened to a rigid, aluminum-girdered external skeleton covered by fabric. The control cabin, engines, and maneuvering surfaces were distributed along and suspended from this load-carrying frame thereby not only making higher speeds possible, but eliminating as well the problems hitherto caused when winds and aerodynamic forces deformed the surfaces of the uncontained gas bags. By 1910 aerial passenger service by Zeppelin in Germany had become a reality. Passengers comfortably seated in wicker chairs on pile rugs were served wine and cold lunches; but their travel was not without its risks. More than half of the twenty-six dirigibles built by Count von Zeppelin by 1914 had come to a violent end.

The two most famous of the rigid airships were the *Hindenburg* and her earlier sister airship, the *Graf Zeppelin*, and it was the successful commercial exploitation of these two giant airships that kept lighter-than-air aviation alive. Passengers paid $720 apiece for a round-trip ticket between Germany and the United States and cruised in luxury at a stately 78 mph during the voyage. The *Hindenburg* made ten round trips between New York and Germany in 1936; and then on May 3, 1937, ninety-six persons boarded the Zeppelin for its first flight to New York of the 1937 season. The crossing was prolonged by headwinds and in the New York area thunderstorms delayed the landing, but finally on May 6, a little after seven P.M., the Hindenburg approached its mooring mast at Lakehurst, New Jersey, dropped its cables and suddenly, without warning, disaster struck. Sheets of flame enveloped the tail section; the exploding hydrogen leapt high in the air, the massive skeleton buckled, girders twisted in the raging heat; and as horrified spectators and newscasters watched, passengers flung themselves out of the flaming airship as it crumpled like some huge, mortally wounded animal to the ground. Thirty-five of its ninety-six passengers and crew were killed, countless others were terribly burned. The spectacle of the catastrophe was so appalling that the end of the *Hindenburg* marked the end of the Zeppelin era.

World War I Aviation

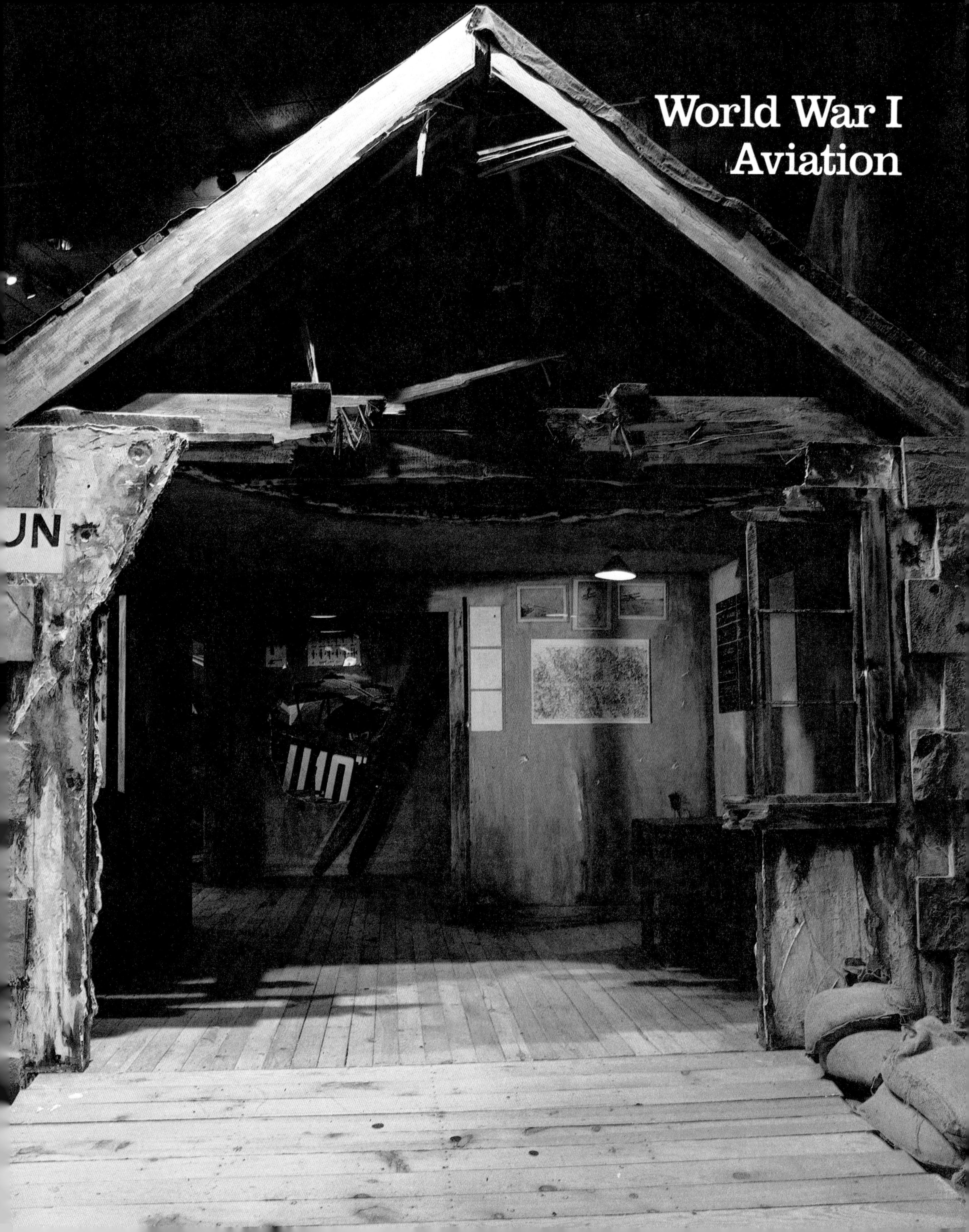

The Museum's SPAD VII in mid-victory roll wears the Indian-head insignia of the famed Escadrille Lafayette N. 124.

In 1914, when World War I began, the airplane was still a crude, powered "box kite" of dubious structural strength and reliability. Although there were aircraft that could fly 125 miles per hour, or travel non-stop over hundreds of miles, or attain an altitude of 19,800 feet, no one machine could accomplish all of these feats, and an aircraft capable of high performance in one area was usually too specialized to perform well in another.

Both sides initially used the aircraft for observation. A slow, stable aerial platform was needed from which an observer or pilot could study or photograph enemy movements, troop disposition, and activities on the ground. "When we started the First World War," recalled T.O.M. Sopwith, the British aircraft designer and builder, "there were no fighters. The small, rather high-performance—for their day—aircraft that we were building were really built as scouts. From scouts they developed into fighters, literally—from going up with rifles and revolvers to the day when we learned to fire through the propeller." The pressure the outbreak of the war created upon the

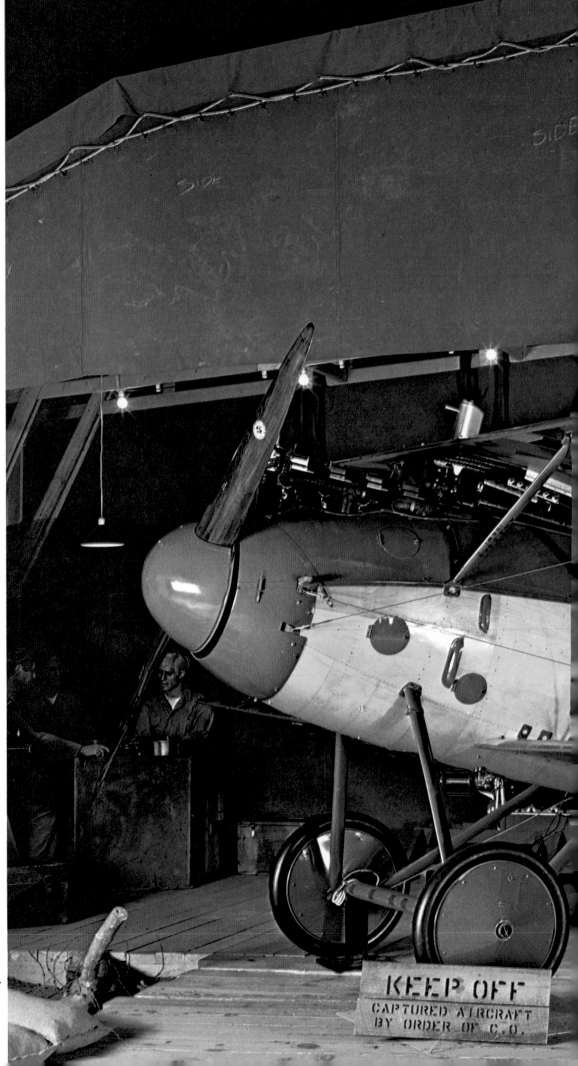

An Albatros D.Va, one of two remaining in the world, sits in front of the Museum's recreation of a World War I forward airfield's primitive hangar tent.

designers of aircraft to come up with new machines of advanced design and greater capabilities was enormous. "Development was so fast!" Sopwith commented. "We literally thought of and designed and flew the airplanes in a space of about six or eight weeks.... From sketches the designers went to chalk on the wall. Until about the middle of the war there was no stressing at all. Everything was built entirely by eye. That's why there were so many structural failures. We didn't start to stress airplanes at all seriously until the [Sopwith] Camel in 1917." The rapid, alternating, and increasingly sophisticated technological advancements made by both sides in aerial tactics, weaponry, aircraft performance and design were brought about by the opposing forces' determination to deny each other the advantages of aerial observation. Therefore, by 1917 the crude "box kite" had developed into a relatively reliable aerobatic weapon capable of shooting down its opponents.

The National Air and Space Museum's aim in creating the World War I Aviation exhibit is to present some of the facts and artifacts appropriate to that period in an environment created to enhance the Museum visitor's appreciation of what it might have been like at an Allied advance airstrip near Verdun, France, during that war.

The Museum exhibit's setting was reconstructed from available records and interviews; the specimens are authentic, the facts correct for the date and event depicted—the few hours following the actual capture by American pilots of Lt. Freiherr Heinz von Beaulieu-Marconnay's brand-new Fokker D.VII, the "U-10," just two days before the signing of the Armistice that ended World War I.

The sky was sodden, patchy with fog. Rain was falling that cold November 9, 1918, morning, as it had been ever since the detachment from First Flight of the First Pursuit Group's 95th Aero Squadron had been ordered to the small forward airfield just east of the ruins of Verdun. Although the French army continued to block the German advance on Verdun, the city's buildings had been shattered and burned by years of German artillery fire. The Meuse-Argonne-St. Mihiel offensive was in its final days. To the east a French infantry division and elements of the American 81st Division were engaging the Germans near Moranville. Far to the north and west Pershing's army had pushed the enemy back to the Meuse line and the outskirts of Sedan. The German army was in general retreat all along the western front; a revolution was threatening in Germany itself. The detachment of First Flight had been ordered up to the advance airfield to destroy German observation balloons and any low-flying German observation aircraft attempting to sneak across the lines should a break in the weather occur. Because of the fog, heavy sporadic rains, and overcast skies of the past few days, however, German air activity had almost completely ceased.

Living conditions at the advance base were primitive. The pilots were housed in two shell-pocked, aged buildings; the unit's SPADs were tucked inside two hangars built and abandoned long before by the French. German artillery and anti-aircraft guns were dug in just behind a ridge to the east and the northeast of the airfield. The base had been hit a number of times in previous months by German artillery fired not at the airfield but at the huge 16-inch U.S. Naval guns five hundred yards south of the rudimentary runway. These Naval guns were mounted on railroad trucks and wheeled out on spurs of track just to the south and west of the field when they were to be fired. Captain Alexander H. McLanahan, A.S., U.S.A., who was in command of the First Flight detachment recalls that the

two American Naval guns went off at regular intervals of 20 minutes day and night. These tremendous pieces must be heard to be appreciated. They caused such terrific displacement of the air when they exploded that our ships were gradually being shaken to pieces. It was impossible to keep the wings in line or the wires tight. Neither could the pilots sleep with continual explosions which almost bounced them from their beds and shook their very teeth out. Plates of food jumped all over the table unless held down and packs of cards flew about like swallows every time the guns went off. To add to it all the German artillery was constantly trying to land shells on the American battery, many of which fell short here and there about the airdrome and barracks. Despite all, we carried on until we began to fall asleep while walking about.

Due to the sporadic artillery bombardment and continuing bad weather no flight operations had been scheduled that morning and the detachment's SPAD XIII aircraft had been withdrawn out of sight within the hangars. Detachment Commander McLanahan, Flight Commander Lt. Edward P. Curtiss, and Lt. Sumner Sewall were playing cards in their barracks when, according to McLanahan's recollection,

> we suddenly heard a strange sounding plane— not like any of ours. Upon looking out the window we saw this Fokker flying very low and circling the field. We grabbed our revolvers—as in my case with the playing cards still in my left hand—and we dashed out and waved to the plane to come down. To our astonishment he did, and we were able to surround him. The three of us with our revolvers had captured him before he could set fire to his plane.
>
> Upon questioning the German pilot, he said he was flying this brand-new Fokker from the rear to the Metz airdrome but apparently got lost. He said he had been flying on the British front and was not familiar with our territory.... When the pilot found he was captured he appeared to turn philosophical and said that after all the war would soon be over.

The German pilot, Lt. Freiherr Heinz von Beaulieu-Marconnay, of the 65th Jagdstaffel was, Lt. Sumner Sewall later recalled, "welcomed with an appropriate shot of Cognac and good fellowship, after which we turned him over to the nearby artillery outfit for further processing."

Over the years since the Fokker D.VII became the possession of the Smithsonian, speculation has centered upon why von Beaulieu-Marconnay gave up so readily and what the possible significance might have

been of the "U-10" painted in such large white block letters on both sides of the Fokker's fuselage between the cockpit and the Roman cross and over the center section of the upper surface of the top wing. The answer to the first question appears to be that the German pilot might easily have mistaken the advance airdrome for one behind the German lines; von Beaulieu-Marconnay was admittedly lost, no Allied aircraft were visible on the field, and the German pilot, once down on the ground and having recognized his mistake, seemed depressed and did not appear to care where he had landed, according to Detachment Commander McLanahan and Lt. Sewall. It was subsequently learned that the pilot's older brother, Lt. Freiherr Oliver von Beaulieu-Marconnay (winner of Germany's highest decoration, *Pour le Mérite*... for his twenty-five aerial victories) had been shot down in combat that October 18th and had died of his wounds on the 30th, just twelve days before Freiherr Heinz von Beaulieu-Marconnay dropped out of that gray November sky to land at the 95th Aero Squadron's advance airbase.

The mystery of the enigmatic "U-10" was solved when a careful search into von Beaulieu-Marconnay's military records turned up the fact that prior to his service as a pilot he had served with one of Germany's most prestigious cavalry regiments: the 10th Uhlans.

The Fokker D.VII flown by von Beaulieu-Marconnay was one of the best single-seat fighter aircraft produced during the war and was said to make good pilots out of poor ones. Although the D.VII was not as fast as the SPAD or the S.E.5, it was responsive and easy to control all the way to its ceiling. Its ability to hold a steep climbing angle without stalling made it especially dangerous in the favored attacking angle of coming in from the rear and below. And when the D.VII did stall, its nose dipped forward without the plane falling off into a spin. Since the D.VII could attain and maintain a higher altitude than most Allied

machines it was able to drop down on
unsuspecting aircraft with lethal results.
The Fokker D.VII was so feared and
respected by Allied airmen that the
surrender of all this specific model of
German aircraft was incorporated into the
Armistice terms.

The two Allied aircraft in this gallery are
both Spads—an acronym for *Société pour
Appareils Deperdussin*, or, in rough
translation, the Deperdussin Aeroplanes
Society. Armand Deperdussin had been the
founder, but he had resigned as head of the
firm before the war and been replaced by
Louis Blériot, the famous French aviator.
Blériot had changed the name of the firm to
Société pour Aviation et ses Dérives [Society
for Aviation and its Derivatives] so its initials
remained the same. The SPAD was probably
the most famous aircraft of World War I
and the SPAD VII, hanging upside down
in the gallery as though in inverted flight,
was considered a very "hot" machine.
They were noted for their high rate of climb
and rugged construction which
enabled them to dive at high speeds without
losing their wings—a not uncommon
accident with other aircraft. Although the
SPAD VII was a favorite with good pilots, it was
a very tricky plane to handle at low speeds
because of its very steep gliding angle with

General "Billy" Mitchell's two-seater SPAD
XVI was filled with Scarff ring-mounted twin
Lewis machine guns—but this model SPAD
was never popular with pilots. The osprey
insignia was Mitchell's own.

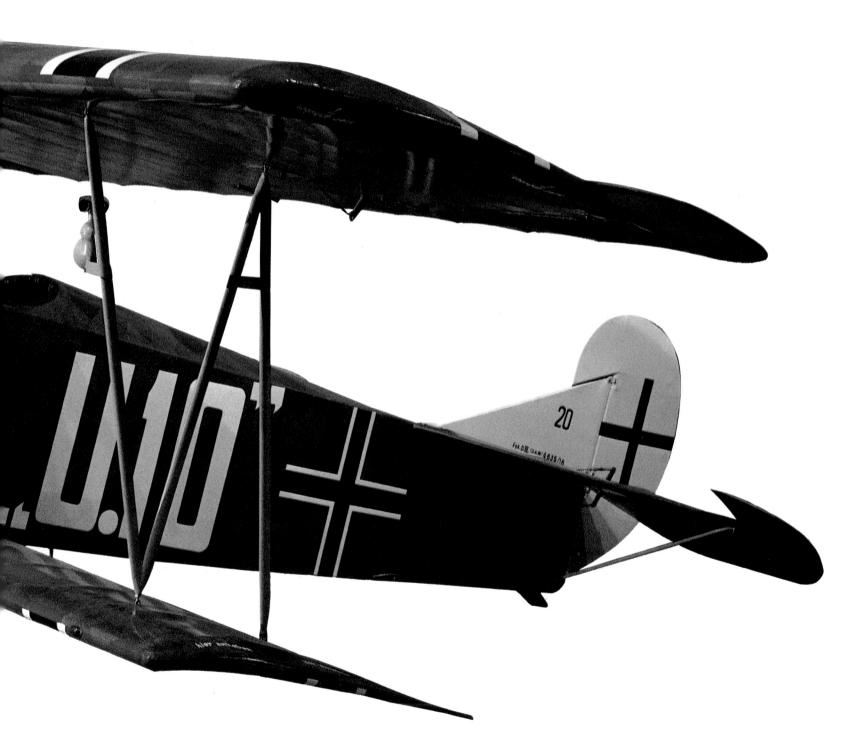

The Fokker D.VII was so respected by World War I Allied airmen that its surrender was specified in the Armistice agreements.

power-off, a rather technical way of saying that without its engine it dropped like a brick. Pilots landing them had to "fly them onto the ground," with their power on. Many fatalities occurred when the engine quit just after take-off or on landing approaches. The Museum's specimen carries the Indian head insignia of the famed Escadrille Lafayette, the unit with which American pilots first saw combat during the war. James Norman Hall, who with Charles Nordhoff was the author of *Mutiny on the Bounty*, served with the Escadrille. Hall, again with Nordhoff, wrote one of the best books to come out of that experience. Here in this excerpt from his *Falcons of France* he tells of his first impressions of aerial combat:

> While in training in the schools I had often tried to imagine what my first air battle would be like. I haven't a very fertile imagination, and in my mental picture of such a battle I had seen planes approaching one another more or less deliberately, their guns spitting fire, then turning to spit again. That, in fact, is what happens, except that the approach is anything but deliberate once the engagement starts. But where I had been chiefly mistaken was in thinking of them fighting at a considerable distance from each other—two, or three, or even five hundred yards. The reality was far different. At the instant when I found myself surrounded by planes, I heard unmistakably the crackle of machine-gun fire. It is curious how different this sounds in the air when one's ears are deafened by altitude, the rush of wind, and the roar of the motor. Even when quite close it is only a faint crackle, but very distinct, each explosion impinging sharply on the eardrums. I turned my head over my shoulder, to breathe the acrid smoke of tracer bullets, and just then—whang! crash!—my wind shield was shattered. I made a steep bank in time to see the black crosses of a silver-bellied Albatros turned up horizontally about twenty yards distant, as though the German pilot merely wanted to display them to convince me that he was really a German. Then, as I leveled off, glancing hastily to my right, I saw not ten metres below my altitude and flying in the same direction a craft that looked enormous, larger than three of mine. She had staggered wings, and there was no doubt about the insignia on her fishlike tail: that too was a black cross. It was a two-seater, and so close that I could clearly see the pilot and the gunner in the back seat. Body and wings were camouflaged, not in daubs after the French fashion, but in zigzag lines of brown and green. The observer, whose back was toward me, was aiming two guns mounted on a single swivel on the circular tract surrounding his cockpit. He crouched down, firing at a steep angle at someone overhead whom I could not see, his tracers stabbing through the air in thin clear lines. Apparently neither the pilot nor the rear gunner saw me. Then I had a blurred glimpse of the tri-color *cocardes* of a Spad that passed me like a flash, going in the opposite direction; and in that same instant I saw another Spad appear directly under the two-seater, nose up vertically, and seem to hang there as though suspended by an invisible wire.
>
> What then happened is beyond the power of any words of mine to describe. A sheet of intense flame shot up from the two-seater, lapping like water around the wings and blown back along the body of the plane. The observer dropped his guns and I could all but see the expression of horror on his face as he turned. He ducked for a second with his arms around his head in an effort to protect himself; then without a moment's hesitation he climbed on his seat and threw himself off into space. The huge plane veered up on one side, turned nose down, and disappeared beneath me. Five seconds later I was alone. There wasn't another plane to be seen.

—*Falcons of France*, by James Norman Hall and Charles Nordhoff

No Allied pilots and, until near the end of the war, very few Germans carried parachutes. The pack parachute did exist; it had been invented by an American showman before the war, but only spotters in observation balloons were equipped with them. The reasons for not giving parachutes to pilots were both cruel and stupid. The excuses were that parachutes were not reliable enough to justify mass production of them and that if a pilot wore a parachute he might be tempted to use it instead of committing himself to the fight. Hall's account of the observer leaping to his death was not an uncommon occurrence. Most pilots were more afraid of fire than bullets and would jump from their burning aircraft, choosing the quick certainty of that death to slowly burning alive.

One of the most famous airmen of World War I was Manfred von Richthofen, the Red Baron, Germany's leading ace who shot down 80 Allied planes. In this excerpt from his autobiography he describes his battle with a British aircraft in April, 1917:

Suddenly one of the impertinent Englishmen tried to drop down upon me. I allowed him to approach me quite near, and then we started a merry quadrille. Sometimes my opponent flew on his back and sometimes he did other tricks. He was flying a two-seater fighter. I realized very soon that I was his master and that he could not escape me.

During an interval in the fighting I assured myself that we were alone. It followed that the victory would belong to him who was calmest, who shot best, and who had the cleverest brain in a moment of danger. Soon I had got him beneath me without having seriously hurt him with my gun. We were at least two kilometers from the front. I thought he intended to land, but there I had made a mistake. Suddenly, when he was only a few yards above the ground, I noticed how he once more went off on a straight course. He tried to escape me. That was too bad.

I attacked him again, and to do so I had to go so low that I was afraid of touching the roofs of the houses in the village beneath me. The Englishman defended himself up to the last moment. At the very end I felt that my engine had been hit. Still I did not let go. He had to fall. He flew at full speed right into a block of houses.

There is little left to be said. This was once more a case of splendid daring. The man had defended himself to the last. However, in my opinion he showed, after all, more stupid foolhardiness than courage. It was again one of the cases where one must differentiate between energy and idiocy. He had to come down in any case, but he paid for his stupidity with his life.

—Captain Manfred Freiherr von Richthofen, trans. by T. Ellis Barker

Not all fighter pilots were as cold-blooded as von Richthofen. Gill Robb Wilson, who flew with both the French and the American air service during World War I recalled the following incident which indicates the occasional startling intimacy of aerial combat:

I was out one day flying as gunner with a friend of mine named Jean Henin. He was kind of a clown, but a very nice boy; he'd been a bank clerk in Paris. We got into a dog fight over the Oise canal. I was firing to the rear. Suddenly I felt Henin beating me on the back, and I could hear him yelling, "Here, over here! Fire, fire!"

I turned around—I had to swing the Lewis guns—and there with his wings locked with ours was a German fighter in a Pfalz. I looked right down this German's throat. He was a man, I would think about forty-five or fifty years old. He had on a black woolen helmet. How in God's name he ever got there I don't know. I could touch the end of his wing.

I swung the guns on him, and the guy just sat there. He had a mustache. I can still see him. There were deep lines on his face, and he looked at me with a kind of resignation. I looked over those machine guns at that guy, and I couldn't kill him. He was too helpless.

Gradually, he drifted off. I said to Henin, "I couldn't kill him." He said, "I'm glad you didn't."

—Oral History Collection of Columbia University

Legends have arisen over the accomplishments of some of the World War I aces with the passage of time, but most historians agree that the role played by air power during this struggle was more romantic than decisive. The most important missions the airplane carried out were reconnaissance and artillery fire control. And when the war bogged down into static frontline trench warfare and increasingly effective camouflage techniques evolved, aerial reconnaissance became less and less significant. No airplane or Zeppelin sank or even seriously disabled any major naval vessel. No war industry was halted by strategic bombing. No major battle's outcome was decided by either control of the air or lack of its control. And so, even though vast technical progress was made in aviation development during World War I, what one celebrates are the men and not so much the machines. Men like Baron Manfred von Richthofen, a brilliant organizer and tactical leader; René Fonck, the leading French ace with 75 victories who would later fail in his attempt to beat Lindbergh across the Atlantic; Britain's Albert Ball, 44 victories, who planted vegetables and raised rabbits around the airfield and who reassured his parents in writing that he was still saying his prayers. Ball died before he reached twenty; one day he simply disappeared. So did Georges Guynemeyer, France's second leading ace. And there was Willy Coppens, the Belgian ace who, incredible as it may seem, actually rolled his wheels on the top of a German observation balloon. Edward Mannock, Britain's top ace with 73 victories, was killed by a German infantryman's rifle bullet. Billy Bishop of Canada survived the war with 72 victories and the Victoria Cross for singlehandedly attacking a German airfield. Eddie Rickenbacker, a former racing car driver and General Pershing's chauffeur, became America's leading ace with 26 victories between the end of April and October, 1918—three months of which he was hospitalized and unable to fly. It is especially fitting that one section of the gallery is devoted to memorabilia pertaining to the Escadrille Lafayette, the famed American volunteer unit that flew for the French at the outbreak of the war. It is a celebration tempered, however, with sorrow, a sadness recognized by a dismayed Orville Wright himself, who in 1917 wrote, "When my brother and I built the first man-carrying flying machine we thought that we were introducing into the world an invention which would make further wars practically impossible."

A SPAD awaiting restoration at the Silver Hill, Maryland, facility.

Flight Technology

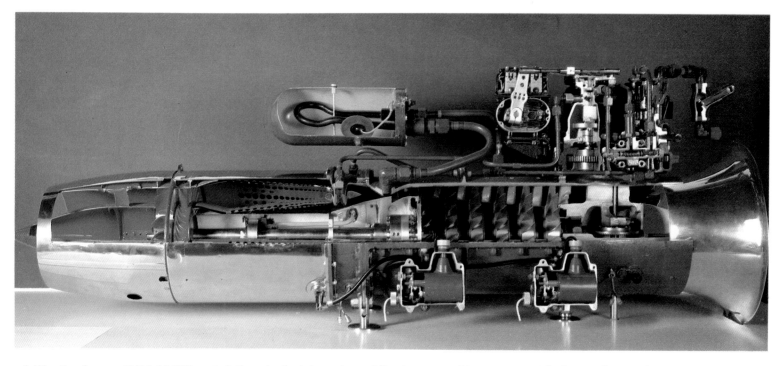

A Westinghouse 9.5A (J-32) axial-flow turbojet engine of the type used to power guided missiles and target drones.

As the visitor to the National Air and Space Museum's Hall of Flight Technology approaches the gallery entrance he is greeted by a series of panels upon which somewhat lyrical quotations from Lord Byron and Le Corbusier appear beside Wilbur Wright's splendidly humble observation: "It is possible to fly without motors, but not without skill. This I conceive to be fortunate, for man, by reason of his greater intellect, can more reasonably hope to equal birds in knowledge, than to equal nature in the perfection of her machinery."

The visitor is then immediately introduced to cardboard cut-out figures of Wheeler King and Ace Blue, two young boys dressed in 1900s clothing, who are watching the flight of a 1908 Wright aircraft. "I'm going to grow up and build the best airplanes in the whole world," says Wheeler King. "You build them," replies Ace Blue, "and I'll fly them and go faster and higher than anybody." Wheeler and Ace will become the visitor's guides to

the Flight Technology hall and their appearance throughout provides the continuity as the visitor moves through the various exhibit units in the gallery.

Surveys conducted by the National Air and Space Museum revealed that the majority of its visitors are either completely unfamiliar with the basic tenets of flight or, at least, relatively misinformed. Most visitors believe that a particular airplane was the result of one visionary individual's determination to build that specific machine rather than, in reality, the aircraft being the product of an intimate partnership of scientists, engineers, skilled technicians, test pilots, and designers.

Because the technology that underlies aircraft design and development is essential to the success of the vehicle, and because the necessity for this technology remains either misunderstood or almost totally unappreciated by the average Museum visitor, the Flight Technology gallery is an overt effort on the part of the NASM staff to educate the public. By explaining the contributions made by the various technological specialties in the development and production of a flying machine and by demonstrating, in addition to explaining, the principles of flight, the Museum hopes that the visitor will achieve a greater understanding and appreciation of flight technology in as painless a manner as possible.

Since the Museum staff recognized that most visitors would find it tedious to follow any extensive written technical presentation—especially when the subject matter involved specialized areas—they wisely decided to discard the conventional museum use of labels in favor of graphics, audio-visual presentations, and puppet theater shows.

Explanations follow of the four forces of aircraft flight: Lift, Thrust, Weight, and Drag. (The practical application of the forces of *lift* and *thrust* results in powered flight. *Thrust*'s forward action creates motion, this motion results in *drag;* the forward motion also enables the wing to produce *lift,* which overcomes the downward pull of *weight.*) Short animated films demonstrate and explain how lift functions, that an aircraft's control surfaces are deflected to vary the

Howard Hughes stands beside his Hughes H-1 Racer in which, on September 13, 1935, he set a world speed record of over 352 mph.

direction and intensity of lift. A film explains the three-dimensional world in which an aircraft operates and how its movement within this world is defined about three axes: yaw, pitch, and roll. A propeller is shown to be nothing more complicated than a wing with a twist.

The visitor is then directed to the propulsion exhibit, which contains the Museum's "dancing engine": a Pratt and Whitney R-985 Wasp junior radial piston engine that has been sliced through the middle to expose its cylinders and inner working parts. The engine on display, taken from a Navy airplane that had flown many hours, is driven now by a hidden electric motor. As the visitor watches, the two halves of the engine separate and pirouette around and apart to display its working pistons and such important components as the piston rings, inlet and exhaust valves, valve springs, connecting rods, master rod, and counterweights. The nine cylinders are arranged in a circle around the crankshaft. The ease with which a radial engine could be maintained and serviced was one of its most important features; each cylinder could be removed separately for service without having to take apart the rest of the engine.

Also part of the propulsion exhibit unit is the Caldwell variable-pitch constant-speed propeller. A variable-pitch constant-speed propeller makes it possible for the engine to operate at the optimum revolutions per minute regardless of flight conditions, thus increasing propeller efficiency and reducing engine wear. By increasing the pitch of a propeller—the angle at which the propeller blade strikes the air—one obtains higher efficiency without increasing the speed of the engine. Equally important was the development of the supercharger, which made it possible for piston engines to operate efficiently at high altitudes; and not far from the Caldwell variable-pitch propeller is a cut-away General Electric supercharger of the sort used on a Boeing B-17 Flying Fortress heavy bomber during World War II.

A more advanced propulsion system

utilizing some of the principles of both the internal combustion engine and the supercharger is a turbojet. Here the power developed by a turbine is used to drive a compressor that supplies air to a burner. Hot gases from the burner pass through the turbine and from there continue rearward through the thrust-producing exhaust nozzle.

There is only one actual airplane in the Flight Technology gallery: the Hughes H-1 racer. And although there might arguably be other famous aircraft more deserving of galleries all to themselves, the H-1's inclusion is due to its being such a superb example of an airplane regarded as an excellent solution to a design problem. And besides, the Hughes racer is one of the most beautiful airplanes built at any time, anywhere. The H-1, designed by Richard Palmer, built by Glenn Odekirk, and piloted by Howard Hughes, was developed to be the fastest landplane in the world. Noah Dietrich, who was chief executive officer of the Howard Hughes empire for thirty-two years, recalls

Movie stunt flyer Paul Mantz and Amelia Earhart witnessed Howard Hughes' successful speed-record attempt.

the summer day in 1935 when the H-1 was wheeled out into the sunlight for the first time:

. . . Howard [Hughes] announced that he was going to be the first pilot to take it up.

This was not what I would have liked. It also concerned Odekirk and Palmer. No one could say for certain that it would fly successfully. But Howard insisted that he was going to be the one to find out.

It performed beautifully. And fast. Faster than the observers had ever seen an airplane travel. Howard decided immediately he would try for the land-plane speed record.

The test was scheduled for September 12, 1935 at Martin Field at Santa Ana. Howard invited me down for the event, and I had my usual queasiness watching him fly. He made a try at the record that day, but darkness fell before he could finish the four runs. The test was postponed until the following day—Friday the 13th.

Fliers of those days were a superstitious lot, and some of Howard's fellow aviators tried to dissuade him from a Friday the 13th flight. Howard had phobias galore, but no superstitions. Friday the 13th was just another flying day to him.

The device for timing Howard's flights was complicated. It had been developed by Western Union and it featured two electrically timed clocks a mile apart, connected by wire. Two cameras were aimed at the clocks and tilted so they would also photograph the plane passing overhead. The plane had to be flown at 200 feet so that the identifying number on the wing would show in the photograph.

Howard took off in the H-1. Circling overhead to observe his feat were two friends, Amelia Earhart and Paul Mantz, the movie stunt flier. Howard pushed the H-1 to the extreme in four passes over the course, and all of us watching him realized that he was breaking the record.

He wasn't satisfied. He wanted to test the utmost capacity of his plane, and he zoomed up to 12,000 feet, then nosed downward and hurtled toward the earth.

My heart was in my throat as I watched that little plane speed relentlessly toward the ground. He pulled out of the dive just as he reached the timing course and streaked past the observers.

Then the engine conked out.

The plane was speeding away from the

landing field at low altitude. I saw it zoom up to 1800 feet and then dip down to earth.

Everyone leaped into cars and headed for the bean field where the plane had disappeared. We arrived to find Howard stepping jauntily from the H-1. He had scarcely a scratch, and the plane suffered little damage.

His feat made headlines around the world; a new land-plane speed record of 352.39 miles per hour, almost 40 miles per hour faster than the previous mark.

After the record flight there was speculation in the press about the cause of the crash. One report declared that a piece of steel wool had been discovered in the fuel line, and there were hints of sabotage. Not true. Howard had simply run out of gas. He had gone up with a minimum load to limit the plane's weight. Odekirk had warned him to keep a careful eye on the gas gauge, but Howard had forgotten to.

—HOWARD, *The Amazing Mr. Hughes*
by Noah Dietrich with
Bob Thomas

The Hughes racer had two sets of wings; the wings on the aircraft as displayed are the long set measuring 31′9″ and have a moderate aspect ratio. They were used on January 19, 1937, when Hughes broke the transcontinental speed record. He left Los Angeles before dawn and arrived outside New York City at Newark Airport 7 hours, 28 minutes and 25 seconds later. He traveled the 2,490-mile course at an average speed of 332 mph. The wings Hughes used for the landplane record flight witnessed by Noah Dietrich were of a low-aspect ratio and about six feet shorter than the wings displayed.

The "long-winged" version of the Hughes Racer—one of the Museum's most beautiful aircraft.

Although the Hughes H-1 racer was specifically designed for record-setting purposes, it had a great impact on the design of high-performance aircraft for years to come. Some of the H-1's outstanding design features were:

1) A close-fitting, bell-shaped engine cowling that reduced airframe drag and improved engine cooling.

2) Gently curving wing fillets between the wing and the fuselage to help stabilize airflow, reduce drag, and prevent potentially dangerous eddying and tail buffeting.

3) A retractable landing gear—so perfectly fitted that visitors must look hard to determine where the gear fairings and doors merge with the bottom of the wing—to reduce drag and increase speed and range.

4) All rivets and joints flush with the aircraft's aluminum skin, and plywood wings with flathead and countersunk screws.

5) Ailerons that droop 15° when the flaps are fully extended. This increases lift along the full span of the wings during takeoff and landing.

6) A smoothly faired and totally enclosed cockpit, in which the pilot sits.

The H-1 demonstrated that properly designed radial-engine aircraft could compete with the lower-drag in-line designs despite the large frontal areas required by radial-engine installation; and the Hughes racer was a major milestone on the road to such later high-performance radial-engined World War II fighters as the American Grumman F6F Hellcat and Republic P-47 Thunderbolt as well as the Japanese Mitsubishi Type 0 (Zero) and Germany's Focke-Wulf FW-190.

The remaining unit exhibits reinforce the visitor's understanding of the manner in which flight technology has responded, expanded, and necessarily continued to make compromises in order to produce advanced aircraft capable of performing ever more demanding functions. Emphasis shifts now to the problems encountered when aerodynamic flight moves into the transonic (the transition area of speeds below and above the speed of sound) and supersonic (faster than the speed of sound; i.e., above approximately 738 mph at sea level) regions, as well as the problems encountered in missile development and space flight. Advanced materials, many of which had previously been considered undesirable for flight application, plus unconventional construction methods were required to withstand the kinetic heating experienced in supersonic flight and reentry as well as to provide stability and thermal control in space vehicles.

A mock briefing in a fairy tale about a royal family whose son's experiments with balloons lead to the development of a jet-propelled royal carriage helps the visitor understand the principles of jet propulsion. Exhibits and audio-visual displays demonstrate how the principles of jet propulsion are used in turbojet, turbofan, and ramjet engines; and then the principles of rocketry are developed through comparison with jet propulsion. The final puppet theater presentation takes place in the Advanced Space Technology Theater where we find Wheeler King explaining to Ace Blue, both now retired and elderly gentlemen, why the refinements in technology have been necessary; how Ace, who longs for the "good old days," should appreciate the extraordinary space age accomplishments that these advances have achieved, such as ITOS and GOES weather monitoring satellites and the LANDSAT earth survey satellite; how photovoltaic (solar) cells on Skylab's one wing produced approximately 5,000 watts of electricity; and that the new construction materials created out of pyrolized carbon fibers in a carbon matrix used on the space shuttle's fuselage could take a temperature of 3,000°F again and again. Ace becomes a more informed and appreciative individual as a result, and that is exactly what NASM hopes to have achieved with the average Museum visitor through its Flight Technology gallery.

Flight Testing

If the visitor to the Flight Testing gallery comes away with nothing more than an awareness that a test pilot is a highly skilled aerospace professional and *not* the reckless, devil-may-care, high guts to low brain ratio "show-me-where-the-stick-is-and-I'll-fly-it" character depicted by the Hollywood movies of the 1930s, then one of the primary purposes of this gallery has been realized.

More than fifty years ago Edward P. Warner and F. H. Norton of the National Advisory Committee for Aeronautics (NACA, the National Aeronautics and Space Administration's forerunner) wrote: "Test flying is a highly specialized branch of work, the difficulties of which are not generally appreciated and there is no type of flying in which a difference between the abilities of pilots thoroughly competent in ordinary flying becomes more quickly apparent." The main aim of the Flight Testing gallery—also known as the Hall of X-Airplanes, "X" for Experimental—is to demonstrate the importance of the test pilot's work to the development of new aircraft and to the derivation of new knowledge in the aeronautical sciences.

In the Early Flight gallery one can find the 1894 Lilienthal glider, one of eight machines of this type built by that towering figure of early flight testing, Otto Lilienthal himself, whose studies of the lift created by a curved surface on a moving stream of air, *Der Vogelflug als Grundlage der Fliegekunst* [Bird Flight as the Basis of Aviation], had such an influence on the Wright brothers' work.

In 1896 Lilienthal wrote, "One can get a proper insight into the practice of flying only by actual flying experiments." Otto Lilienthal was fully aware of the risks involved testing flying machines, but, as he said shortly before his fatal accident, "Sacrifices must be made."

Each of the three full-size aircraft on exhibition in this gallery represents a separate aspect of flight research. The first, Wiley Post's modified Lockheed Model 5-C "Vega," the *Winnie Mae*, is displayed with its special jettisonable landing gear and Post's pressure suit used during his high-altitude research flights.

The second aircraft is the Bell XP-59A Airacomet, America's first experimental turbojet-propelled aircraft.

The other aircraft is the Hawker-Siddeley Kestrel, a vertical and short takeoff and landing (V/STOL) research aircraft which is here as a representative of a highly successful approach to vertical flight and jetvectored aircraft.

Flight research is undertaken to determine whether an actual machine's performance is what has been predicted or hoped for through its design, to provide basic information and experience that will benefit aeronautical science in general, to furnish additional data that will be useful in the continuing development of the particular series of aircraft being tested, and to provide "proof of concept" validation through the in-flight testing of new concepts or developments. From the very earliest days of flight the aims of flight research have been the same.

Orville and Wilbur Wright, who combined extensive ground research in their wind-tunnel experiments on the behavior of various types of wings and propellers with flight research aloft, recognized the need for acquiring reliable, verified data. Along with Otto Lilienthal they acknowledged the elemental partnership between ground research and flight testing. Wilbur, who compared the testing of a flying machine to riding "a fractious horse," stated: "If you are looking for perfect safety you will do well to sit on a fence and watch the birds, but if you really wish to learn you must mount a machine and become acquainted with its tricks by actual trial." The Wrights' determination resulted, on December 17, 1903, in man's first successful powered flight. Orville, who was the test pilot on that flight, wrote:

> Wilbur ran at the side, holding the machine to balance it on the track. The machine, facing a 27-mile wind, started very slowly. Wilbur was able to stay with it until it lifted from the track after a forty-foot run. The course of the flight up and down was exceedingly erratic. The control of the front rudder was difficult. As a result, the machine would suddenly rise to about ten feet and then as suddenly dart for the ground. A sudden dart when a little over 120 feet from the point at which it rose into the air, ended the flight. The flight lasted only

twelve seconds, but it was nevertheless the first in the history of the world in which a machine carrying a man had raised itself by its own power into the air in full flight, had sailed forward without reduction of speed, and had finally landed at a point as high as that from which it started.

As Dr. Richard P. Hallion has written, Orville Wright's post-maiden flight analysis "is a model test flight report. It presents the test conditions, a critical examination and analysis of the airplane's stability and control, and finally, a summation of the flight's significance."

If the average Museum visitor knows anything at all about Wiley Post, it is probably only that he was the pilot of the

98

plane that crashed near Point Barrow, Alaska, killing the humorist Will Rogers, on August 15, 1935. And yet Wiley Post, who died with Rogers in that crash, was the first person to make a solo round-the-world flight (July, 1933) and was the winner of aviation's top awards. Post was honored by two New York ticker-tape parades, was received by two Presidents at the White House; he created the world's first practical high-altitude pressure suit, discovered and was the first to take advantage of the jet stream, and at the time of his death had flown more hours at ground speeds above 300 mph and had more flight hours in the stratosphere than any other man. Lauren D. Lyman, then aviation editor of the *New York Times*, observed at Post's death that it was Wiley Post who moved stratospheric flight into the realm of reality. Post did it in the *Winnie Mae*.

Following his round-the-world flights, Wiley Post made several modifications on the *Winnie Mae* to better enable it to make long-distance high-altitude flights. Because he could not pressurize the airplane's cabin, Post asked the B. F. Goodrich Company to help him develop a full-pressure suit he could wear while flying the plane. In spite of the suit being created in response to the

Famed aviator Wiley Post completed two round-the-world record flights in 1931 and 1933 and a series of special high-altitude substratospheric flights in the Winnie Mae, *a modified Lockheed Vega.*

limitations of his aircraft, Post's suit, consisting of three layers (long underwear, an inner black rubber air pressure bladder, and an outer cloth contoured suit), and helmet (containing a special oxygen breathing system and outlets for earphones and a throat microphone) must be considered the ancestor of the sort of full-pressure suits used in the X-15 research aircraft and those worn by the astronauts. The *Winnie Mae* was equipped with a supercharger, a special jettisonable landing gear, and a metal-covered spruce landing skid glued to the bottom of the fuselage. In late July, 1934, Post had declared his intention to fly across the country at an altitude of more than 30,000 feet, thereby to take advantage of the high-altitude winds he knew existed.

After months of preparation Post was ready, and early in the morning on February 22, 1935, he put on his pressure suit and helmet, entered the *Winnie Mae*, and took off into the darkness and dense fog surrounding Burbank, California, for New York. At an altitude of about 200 feet, just before climbing through the clouds, Post jettisoned his landing gear to lighten and streamline his plane and, shortly thereafter, just 31 minutes into the flight, his engine began throwing oil. Post prepared for an emergency landing on Muroc Dry Lake in the Mojave Desert. The *Winnie Mae* was carrying more than 300 gallons of fuel and Post had no way to dump it prior to the forced

Thomas Edison's complaint about the Wright brothers' flight was that no aircraft could be considered truly practical until it could rise from the ground and settle back again, vertically. Using a special "vectored thrust" turbo-fan engine, this 1964 Hawker XV-6A Kestrel could rise straight up, hover, dart away in horizontal flight, slow and settle vertically back down on the ground. The success of the experimental Kestrel led to the development of the world's first Vertical Take-Off and Landing (VTOL) jet fighter, the Hawker Siddeley Harrier now in service with the British Royal Air Force and the U.S. Marine Corps.

landing. In spite of the danger, Post, superb pilot that he was, skillfully glided down to so smooth a landing that H. E. Mertz, who was but 400 yards away tinkering on a wind-powered "sail car," did not even hear the *Winnie Mae* land. When Wiley Post, still wearing his high-altitude full-pressure suit and helmet, walked up to Mertz to ask his help in removing the helmet's rear wing nuts, Mertz nearly fainted in terror. It was subsequently learned that the *Winnie Mae* had been sabotaged; a quart of emery dust

learned that he had covered the 2,035 miles in 7 hours and 9 minutes. That meant that not only had the *Winnie Mae* averaged 279 miles per hour, which was over a hundred miles faster than her normal maximum speed, but that at times the *Winnie Mae* had been traveling as fast as 340 miles per hour! There was no question about it: Wiley Post and his *Winnie Mae* had been in the jet stream. As Stanley R. Mohler, M.D., and

had been placed in the supercharger's air intake the night before the flight. The moment the supercharger was cut in, the emery dust was sucked into the engine where it ground down the piston rings and wreaked such havoc that the engine had to be completely rebuilt. The sabotage had been performed at the instigation of a jealous pilot who thought Post's successes were jeopardizing his own chances for sponsorship.

Three weeks later, on March 15, 1935, Wiley Post took off on a second transcontinental record attempt. One hundred miles east of Cleveland, Post ran out of oxygen and had to turn back. He landed the *Winnie Mae* again on her belly, and after he climbed out and his pressure suit was removed Post

Bobby H. Johnson, Ph.D., wrote for a NASM Smithsonian Annals of Flight monograph, "Within a quarter of a century of Post's high altitude flights, men, women, and children would be hurtling through the stratosphere at almost the speed of sound in the comfortable pressurized cabins of jetliners, wholly ignorant of the frustrating labors of 1934 and 1935, unmindful of the man who met the difficulties in their rudest shapes. Yet every time a contrail runs its white chalkline across the blue, it deserves recollection that it was Wiley Post who pointed the way to putting it there."

Wind-tunnel displays and models are exhibited to demonstrate the importance of ground research and its connection with flight research.

One of the most dramatic examples of how ground research can result, in some cases, in basic changes in an aircraft's design is the exhibit related to the Convair F-102

The direct ancestor of all American jet-propelled airplanes, this historic Bell XP-59A Airacomet was a closely guarded wartime secret when it flew in 1942.

interceptor. When this aircraft completed its initial flight tests in 1954, because of unforeseen high-drag characteristics it could not exceed the speed of sound. Richard Whitcomb's ground research in wind tunnels revealed the value of "area ruling." The NASA scientist's discoveries led to the F-102's having a new "coke bottle" fuselage design, and when this new form was tested, the F-102 handily broke the sound barrier. Flight research thereby validated an important new principle of aircraft design that ground research had discovered. Displayed nearby is a wind-tunnel model of the Bell X-2 tested in 1946 by NACA at the Langley Aeronautical Laboratory's 300 mph wind tunnel. Ten years after wind tunnel tests were begun on this model, after ten years of extended, laborious ground testing resulted in major modifications to its design, this now nearly forgotten research aircraft became on September 27, 1956, the first airplane to fly three times the speed of sound. The Bell X-2 was also the first aircraft to reach an altitude of 126,200 feet.

On the morning of November 20, 1953, piloted by Scott Crossfield, the Douglas D-558-2 Skyrocket, now suspended above the east moving staircase, became the first aircraft to exceed twice the speed of sound.

The stubby-winged Lockheed F-104 Starfighter, hanging above the west moving staircase, was the United States' first interceptor capable of flying at sustained speeds above Mach 2. When the F-104 joined operational fighter squadrons in 1958, it set so many world speed and altitude records, the aircraft was nicknamed "the missile with a man in it."

Vertical Flight

Thomas Edison's comment about the Wright brothers' flight was that no aircraft could be considered truly practical until it could rise from the ground and settle back again, *vertically*. It must then have seemed an impossible task since, as far back as the twelfth century, when the Chinese inserted wooden wings into the top end of a stick, then spun them into the air, men had been trying unsuccessfully to achieve vertical flight. And yet on November 13, 1907, not quite four years after the Wrights' twelve-second flight near Kitty Hawk, a twin rotor-bladed, rigidly trapeze-braced, bicycle-wheeled, and seemingly perfectly symmetrical machine built by Paul Cornu of France developed enough lift to raise itself and its pilot about six feet off the ground for almost twenty seconds. Still, another thirty years would pass before the first fully-controllable helicopter, the Focke-Achgelis FW-61, would fly. This machine was built by Germany's Dr. Heinrich Focke, whose previous experiments with autogiros were evident in the FW-61's design. The Focke-Achgelis FW-61 could achieve a speed of 76 mph and remain aloft for nearly an hour and a half.

Immediately upon entering the gallery the visitor is confronted by a flock of somewhat bizarre-looking machines suspended from wires or atop platforms set at various levels upon the gallery's floor so that one's first image is of an air space crowded with rotor-wing flying machines. This impression reflects the momentary post-World War II euphoric belief that this newly perfected machine was going to become as abundant and commonplace as the automobile and, like the automobile, every family would want to have one. Unfortunately the machines cost too much for mass acceptance.

Near the entrance to the gallery the visitor comes upon illustrations and models of early rotor-wing attempts: a replica of the Chinese "flying top," which was quite possibly the first man-made object designed to fly under its own power. There, too, is a reproduction of one of Leonardo da Vinci's fifteenth-century notebook sketches of a Helix, his proposed helicopter design. Four men would, theoretically, push turn bars attached to a shaft atop which a large "airscrew" was fixed. The men, racing around the circular platform at the Helix's base, would literally screw their machine into the air. Da Vinci was much more fascinated with designing ornithopters (devices with flapping wings) than helicopters, however, and dozens of drawings of ornithopters fill his notebooks. It has been suggested that if Leonardo da Vinci had devoted one-tenth of the attention and time he spent designing ornithopters on inventing fixed-wing gliders instead, he might have developed a working, man-carrying glider four hundred years before Lilienthal.

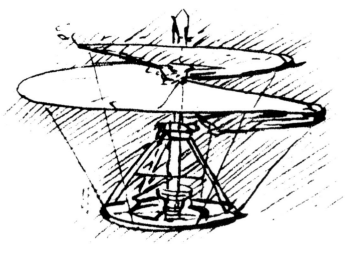

9

Leonardo da Vinci's fifteenth-century sketch of a Helix, a precursor of modern helicopter design.

As the Twentieth Century commenced, full-scale helicopters began to meet with some success as designers from all over the world focused their attention upon the problems of vertical flight. In 1907 two Frenchmen, Louis Breguet and Charles Richet, built the first manned helicopter to leave the ground. Their machine, the Breguet Gyroplane #1, rose about three and a half feet into the air, but assistants placed at each of the machine's four corners were required to provide control and stability. Paul Cornu's helicopter, which rose six feet into the air that same year and did not require tie-down ropes, must be considered the first "successful" helicopter although, like the Breguet Gyroplane, Cornu's helicopter lacked adequate control. In Russia, in 1909, Igor Sikorsky, then twenty years old, built his first helicopter but it lacked power to fly. The following year he built a helicopter that could lift its own weight—but not, regrettably, the additional weight of its pilot. Disillusioned, Sikorsky abandoned helicopters for airplanes and, in 1913, built the world's first four-engined airplane.

Ten years would pass as helicopter inventors continued to be frustrated by their inability to control their machines, and then in 1923, rotor-wing aircraft took a new turn with the development and testing of autogiros.

An autogiro requires the forward pull of a conventionally mounted aircraft engine and propeller to create the moving airstream through which its "lifting wings"—a set of windmilling rotor blades—glide. The important distinction between helicopter blade action and autogiro blade action is that air flows *down* through helicopter blades and *up* through autogiro blades. Juan de la Cierva, a Spaniard, created a successful autogiro in 1923 when he attached flapped hinges to each of his autogiro's four rotor blades, thus providing his machine with the balance and stability essential to helicopter control.

In 1940, Igor Sikorsky returned to the study of helicopters after an absence of thirty years. Now an American citizen and already famous for his multi-engine aircraft and flying boat designs, Sikorsky, in 1941, established a helicopter world endurance record with the VS-300, his first successful helicopter design. Based on this success, the U. S. Army awarded a development contract to Sikorsky for a machine produced in sufficient quantity to fill military needs. The VS-300 led to the XR-4, which completed the first extended cross-country flight by covering 761 miles from the Sikorsky plant in Connecticut to the Wright Field Army Base in Ohio on May 18, 1942. With a few modifications and minor design refinements the XR-4 became the R-4, the first helicopter in the world to enter production. One hundred and thirty-one R-4s were built during World War II and the original XR-4 is now on display in the Vertical Flight gallery.

Among the other major artifacts on display in this gallery is the Kellett XO-60 autogiro, which crouches like some giant insect near the entrance door. An autogiro's ability to provide a slow, stable platform, to fly close enough to the ground for observation, and to make near-vertical takeoffs and landings was quickly recognized as having military potential. In the Kellett autogiro the pilot sat forward of the observer, whose seat could be swiveled to face the front or rear. The cockpit canopy bulged over the fuselage so that the occupants could look down over the sides of the aircraft without sticking their heads into the wind. Windows were also provided in the fuselage floor. After several modifications to the rotor pylon, landing gear, and tail fins, the aircraft was accepted by the Army Air Forces in 1943. Unlike earlier autogiro designs, the Kellett's rotor wing was linked to the engine for "jump" starts. The rotor would be turned to near-takeoff speed, then disconnected while the autogiro was still at rest. With the rotor blades already spinning, the additional normal propeller thrust made a shorter takeoff possible. On the ground the blades could be folded back for easy storage and transport.

A second Sikorsky helicopter in this gallery

Igor Sikorsky's original XR-4 (1942), the first helicopter in the world to enter production.

is his larger UH-34D medium-assault helicopter—a machine familiar to post-Korean War and Vietnam-era servicemen. Designed in 1954 initially for antisubmarine warfare (ASW) and designated the HSS, this design's performance was so outstanding it achieved world speed records: 1,000 kilometers at 141.9 mph; 1,000 kilometers at 132.6 mph. Navy pilots called it the "pushbutton" helicopter since when placed on automatic pilot it would maintain an 80-knot airspeed two hundred feet above the ocean and then, at a preselected spot, automatically dip down to fifty feet, hover and lower its sophisticated sonar gear into the water. The Marines and Army used this type of helicopter for assault missions, wire laying, artillery spotting, medical evacuation, and as a troop and supply transport. A UH-34D in 1961 fished Alan Shepard and his *Freedom 7* spacecraft out of the water following Shepard's first American in space suborbital testing of the Mercury spacecraft.

The Kellett XO-60 autogiro crouches like a giant insect near the Vertical Flight gallery's entrance door.

This event marked the beginning of helicopter use for the recovery of space vehicles. The Museum's specimen wears the markings of Marine Medium Helicopter Squadron 163, a combat unit which served in the Da Nang area of Vietnam in 1965 and was one of the most highly decorated Marine helicopter squadrons of the Vietnam War.

Although the dream of a flying machine in every man's garage has never been realized, visitors to the Vertical Flight gallery emerge with a greater understanding of the variety of uses to which vertical flight aircraft have been put. Helicopter airliners shuttle between this nation's major airports and downtown terminals, eliminating the hassle of crowded rush-hour streets. Helicopters save businessmen time, moving them swiftly from point to point. The helicopters' suitability for rescue work is well known; their ability to hover over otherwise inaccessible areas makes them indispensable for this task.

Young Stanley Hiller, Jr., lands his float-equipped XH-44 in a backyard swimming pool.

The downwash of a helicopter's rotor blades is useful for fighting fires. A helicopter can reach a crash fire-site quickly and once there the downwash helps disperse the heat and flame so that rescuers can approach a crash fire in greater safety. This same downwash evenly distributes agricultural chemicals over foliage and hard-to-reach ground areas. Traffic and police helicopters crisscross over our cities. "Flying cranes" assist in an endless variety of aerial lifting tasks. The military application of helicopters as gunships, air assault weapons, and medical evacuation and supply ships has changed the face of war.

Although the Vertical Flight gallery naturally concentrates on rotor-wing aircraft, other forms of vertical flight are mentioned and shown. The increase in engine thrust-to-weight ratio has made possible vertical flight that is not dependent upon the aerodynamic lift of rotating wings. Several concepts including aircraft with tilt-wings, tilt-props, and directed thrust lift reflect designers' attempts to replace the helicopter—which is limited in forward speed—with high-performance vertical take-off-and-landing (VTOL) machines.

The Vertical Flight gallery touches upon most, if not all, of the many facets by which vertical flight can be achieved. Today all shapes and sizes of helicopters dart like dragonflies through the air. Perhaps, in the not so distant future, a Volkscopter will be developed for everyone's garage; but somehow, the resulting chaos might be one aspect of progress we could do without.

Hiller's Flying Platform was designed as an airborne motorcycle for both military and civilian use.

The Pentecost Hoppicopter was supposed to propel a man up to 80 mph at a maximum altitude of 12,000 feet.

GALLERY
DECK

115 V. OUTLET

April 15th. At sea.

I've never counted how many times a day the bos'n's mates pass the word, but I'd bet we never have 15 consecutive minutes without their "Peeeeep! Now, hear this—" Between sunrise and the end of the working day, we must hear 50 or 60 calls. They are so familiar by now that all we need is the opening phrase; the rest we can supply from memory. As soon as the pipe peeps and the bos'n's mate says, "Turn to!", we know that this will follow: "All sweepers, man your brooms! Clean sweepdown, fore and aft! Empty all trash cans and spit-kits"—delivered in a singsong cadence, with the last syllable of each phrase drawn out and falling.

Here are some of the calls we hear most often:

"All extra-duty men lay down to the master-at-arms' shack."

"General Quarters! General Quarters! All hands man your battle stations on the double!"

"Now, the smoking lamp is out throughout the ship while taking aboard aviation gasoline and fuel oil."

"Relieve the watch!"

"Now five hands from the K division and ten hands from the fifth division report to the First Lieutenant at Number 1 crane."

Pat Garvan told me he knew an officer of the deck who got so fed up with the whole business, he had this word passed: "Now all those who have not done so, do so immediately." My own favorite is, "Now the man with the key to the garbage-grinder lay below and grind same."

—*Aircraft Carrier,* by
Lt. Cmdr. J. Bryan III

The Sea-Air Operations gallery is unquestionably one of the most ambitious exhibits in the National Air and Space Museum since it attempts to recreate the environment of a United States Navy aircraft carrier at sea.

As the Museum visitor approaches the *USS Smithsonian* (CVM-76), a "carrier for all times," he can hear the bos'n's pipes before he even reaches the quarter-deck, the traditional entrance to Navy ships. There he passes between brass stanchions hung with Navy macramé, a highly polished ship's bell glints overhead, the bos'n pipes him aboard, and the visitor finds himself thrust into an aircraft carrier's hangar deck crowded with U. S. Navy and Marine Corps aircraft. All about, one sees actual carrier hangar deck artifacts, wing tanks, munitions, hoses, controls, watertight doors. Stencils direct one's attention to fire extinguishers, lifejackets, safety equipment. No attempt has been made to model the hangar deck after any specific aircraft carrier or period since the airplanes on exhibit span some forty years of Navy flight, but the atmosphere seems to fit more the World War II period than any other.

An aircraft carrier's hangar deck serves primarily as a protected space for working on aircraft, and on an actual ship it is a vast area covering almost two acres that spans the ship's width and nearly two-thirds of its length. During flight operations and peak maintenance hours, a hangar deck is a scene of frenzied activity with aircraft being transferred from the hangar deck to the flight deck by the elevators which extend out from the sides of the ship. The atmosphere in the *Smithsonian's* hangar deck is enhanced by the open hatch against the gallery wall, through which the visitor sees the sea rushing past. A continuous-film loop of about five minutes' duration projects scenes of escort destroyers taking up stations, rescue helicopters returning to the ship. Standing there, one can almost feel the hangar deck heave.

The first aircraft the visitor sees in the hangar deck is a stubby Grumman F4F Wildcat.* The Wildcat was the Navy's and the Marine's best fighter at the outbreak of the

---

*Actually, since the Museum's specimen was manufactured under license by the Eastern Aircraft Division of General Motors, this version was designated FM-1.

Second World War. F4Fs first saw action at Wake Island when that tiny Pacific outpost was attacked on December 8, 1941, and Marine Fighter Squadron VMF-211 lost eight of its twelve F4Fs that first day. For two more weeks the remaining Wildcats fought heroically against the Japanese Zeros, which could outmaneuver and outrun them, and before December 23rd, the day the Japanese landed on Wake Island and the last two Wildcats were destroyed, the Marine's F4Fs even managed to sink a Japanese destroyer and may have sunk a submarine while continuously breaking up air attacks on their island.

Saburo Sakai, Japan's greatest fighter pilot to have survived the war, recalls the day he saw a single Wildcat attacking three Zeros, 1,500 feet below him:

The Zeros should have been able to take the lone Grumman without any trouble, but every time a Zero caught the Wildcat before its guns the enemy plane flipped away wildly and came out again on the tail of a Zero. I had never seen such flying before.

I banked my wings to signal [my wingman] Sasai and dove. The Wildcat was clinging grimly to the tail of a Zero, its tracers chewing up the wings and tail. In desperation I snapped out a burst. At once the Grumman snapped away in a roll to the right, clawed around in a tight turn, and ended up in a climb straight at my own plane. Never had I seen an enemy plane move so quickly or so gracefully before; and every second his guns were moving closer to the belly of my fighter. I snap-rolled in an effort to throw him off. He would not be shaken. He was using my own favorite tactics, coming up from under.

I chopped the throttle back and the Zero shuddered as its speed fell. It worked; his timing off, the enemy pilot pulled back in a turn. I slammed the throttle forward again, rolling to the left. Three times I rolled the Zero, then dropped in a spin, and came out in a left vertical spiral. The Wildcat matched me turn for turn. Our left wings both pointed at a right angle to the sea below us, the right wings to the sky . . . . On the fifth spiral, the Wildcat skidded slightly. I had him, I thought. But the Grumman dropped its nose, gained speed, and the pilot again had his plane in full control. There was a terrific man behind that stick.

He made his error, however, in the next moment. Instead of swinging back to go into a sixth spiral, he fed power to his engine, broke away at an angle, and looped. That was the decisive split second. I went right after him, cutting inside the Grumman's arc, and came out on his tail. I had him. He kept flying loops, trying to narrow down the distance of each arc. Every time he went up and around I cut inside his arc and lessened the distance between our two planes. The Zero could outfly any fighter in the world in this kind of maneuver.

When I was only 50 yards away, the Wildcat broke out of his loop and astonished me by flying straight and level. I pumped 200 rounds into the Grumman's cockpit, watching the bullets chewing up the thin metal skin and shattering the glass . . . the Wildcat continued flying as if nothing had happened. A Zero which had taken that many bullets into its vital cockpit would have been a ball of fire by now. I could not understand it. I slammed the throttle forward and closed in . . . until our planes were flying wing-to-wing formation. I opened my cockpit window and stared out. The Wildcat's cockpit canopy was already back, and I could see the pilot clearly. He was a big man, with a round face. He wore a light khaki uniform. He appeared to be middle-aged, not as young as I had expected.

For several seconds we flew along in our bizarre formation, our eyes meeting across the narrow space between the two planes. The Wildcat was a shambles. Bullet holes had cut the fuselage and wings up from one end to the other. The skin of the rudder was gone, and the metal ribs stuck out like a skeleton. Now I could understand his horizontal flight. Blood stained [the pilot's] right shoulder, and I saw the dark patch moving downward over his chest. It was incredible that his plane was still in the air.

But this was no way to kill a man! Not with him flying helplessly, wounded, his plane a wreck. I raised my left hand and shook my fist at him, shouting, uselessly, I knew, for him to fight instead of just flying along like a clay pigeon. The American looked startled; he raised his right hand weakly and waved.

I had never felt so strange before . . . I honestly didn't know whether I should try to finish him off. Such thoughts were stupid, of course. Wounded or not, he was an enemy, and he had almost taken three of my men a few minutes before. However, there was no reason to aim for the pilot again. I wanted the airplane, not the man.

I dropped back and came in again on his tail . . .

—*Samurai!* by Saburo Sakai
with Martin Caidin

The Boeing F4B-4, one of the best-looking biplane fighters, was the last fixed-landing-gear fighter in the Navy. F4B-4s saw active carrier service until 1937 when they were replaced by Grumman's faster biplane fighters. The Museum's specimen wears the marking of aircraft number 21 Marine Corps Squadron VF-9M. The Army version was designated the P-12.

The Douglas A-4C Skyhawk was sometimes known as "Heinemann's Hot-Rod" after its chief designer, Ed Heinemann, whose philosophy was "simplicate and add lightness." From the late 1950s through the 1960s, the A-4 was the backbone of Navy and Marine Corps light jet attack forces and saw wide use in Vietnam. Unlike many carrier aircraft, the A-4, with its relatively small wingspan (27 1/2 feet), does not have folding wings.

Saburo Sakai set fire to the Wildcat's engine and he saw the pilot bail out and drift down toward the beach at Guadalcanal. Despite the Zero's higher performance, which was made possible by the sacrifice of armor plating, self-sealing fuel tanks, and lighter armament in order to gain long range, good maneuverability, and high speed, in the hands of a skilled pilot the Wildcat could hold its own. It was a tough little fighter and its ratio of victories to losses during World War II was a surprising 6.9 to 1. And even when it was superseded by higher-performance carrier aircraft such as the Grumman F6F Hellcat and the Chance-Vought F4U Corsair, the little Wildcat continued in operation off short-decked escort carriers throughout the war. The cowling on the Museum's F4F was from one of Wake Island's defenders and until the mid-1960s had served as part of the Wake Island Memorial "dedicated to the gallant Marine, Naval, Army and Civilian personnel who defended Wake against overwhelming Japanese invasion armadas, 8 thru 23 December 1941."

Hanging above the Wildcat, as though suspended in flight, is a Douglas SBD-6 Dauntless, the standard Navy dive bomber at the outbreak of the war, whose accurate dive-bombing attacks upon the Japanese fleet during the Battle of Midway resulted in the first major naval defeat suffered by the Japanese. During that battle the Japanese lost four of their ten operational carriers, thereby suffering a blow from which their naval power in the Pacific would never recover. The SBD—its initials stood for Scout Bomber Douglas although its pilots said it was for "Slow But Deadly"—accounted for most of the damage from the air sustained by Japanese aircraft carriers and other surface ships during the war. It was a compact, rugged, and easily serviced aircraft that gave an excellent account of itself in every engagement in which it took part—and it took part in more than was intended since it took longer than expected for its replacement, the Curtiss SB2C, to become acceptable for aircraft carrier service. The

SBD Dauntless could carry a 1,000-pound bomb on its center rack and two 100-pound bombs on wing-mounted racks, all externally mounted. Two .50-caliber machine guns were in the nose and the gunner/observer/radioman had a flexible mount carrying twin .30-caliber machine guns in the rear. Unlike the majority of World War II carrier aircraft, the Dauntless' wings did not fold. NASM's specimen wears the markings of aircraft 109, which served in combat with VS-51 on the USS San Jacinto.

The sporty-looking little biplane suspended from the ceiling behind the Dauntless is a Boeing F4B-4, the last fixed-gear shipboard fighter to see service in the Navy (the Army version of the F4B was the P-12). The F4B first flew in 1928 and went through various design modifications until production of the model displayed in the gallery began in 1932. F4B-4s remained in active carrier service until 1937 when they were replaced by faster biplane fighters built by Grumman. The F4B-4 on exhibit wears the markings of U. S. Marine Squadron VF-9M.

The one jet on the hangar deck floor is a Douglas A-4C whose wingspan, surprisingly, is two and a half feet shorter than the biplane over its head. And yet, despite its relatively small size, the Skyhawk displayed was able to carry some 5,000 pounds of bombs, missiles, fuel tanks, and gun pods in three stations. Later models, beginning with the A-4E, could carry 8,200 pounds in five stations. The A-4 was sometimes known as "Heinemann's Hotrod" after Ed Heinemann of Douglas Aircraft whose design philosophy was "simplicate and add lightness." Because of its small wingspan the A-4 does not have folding wings; elimination of this feature made it possible to build a much lighter plane. The A-4 was the primary Navy and Marine light jet attack plane from the late 1950s through the '60s and its versatility, simplicity, and performance made it a valuable asset to both services. Throughout the Vietnam War the A-4 was noted for its accuracy in attacking selected ground targets. The Museum's specimen wears the markings it wore when it was actually assigned to Navy Attack Squadron VA-76 on board the *USS Bon Homme Richard* while operating off the coast of Vietnam from March to June, 1967. The A-4 is displayed with extra fuel tanks.

After strolling around the aircraft in the hangar deck area, the visitor might ascend to the upper level "balcony" where he can get a different perspective on the planes on display. He would then continue along the balcony platform through a simulated watertight door and continue on into the broad passageway between the PRIFLY (Primary Flight Control) area and the Navigation Bridge.

An aircraft carrier's Navigation Bridge is located high on the forward edge of the carrier's island superstructure and it is the normal duty station of the ship's Commanding Officer during sea operations. From his large swivel chair on the port side of the Bridge the Captain has an unobstructed view of the Flight Deck and the surrounding sea and air space. The Navigation Bridge and the pilot house are open to NASM visitors, and one can stand looking over the Captain's shoulder as jets are catapulted into the air and spotted about the Flight Deck prior to launch. The rear projection movie screens provide an extraordinarily realistic idea of what the bow of an aircraft carrier looks like during air operations.

The PRIFLY section of an aircraft carrier serves essentially the same role as an airport's control tower. Here on the Sea-Air Operations gallery's second level, a visitor can watch aircraft approach the flight deck and make their landings. Like the Navigation Bridge, the PRIFLY area is also equipped with the same radio gear, electronic equipment, and telephones which were taken from actual carriers. Although he is protected from the deafening roar of the jets on the Flight Deck and those making their approaches by walls of armor plate and glass, the visitor can hear what is going on. PRIFLY is the nerve center of a carrier during day operations; it is where the Air Boss can see the entire Flight Deck, from the two steam catapults at the bow all the way back to the stern where the Landing Signal Officer monitors the approaches of the returning aircraft. And while the visitor watches all the landing activity, he can hear the clatter of teletype, radio chatter, the telephones ringing, the Air Boss' orders to the deck crews. From the instant "Launch Aircraft" is ordered by the Air Boss at dawn until the last aircraft has been landed and secured for the night, constant, precise coordination, both physical and mental, is demanded between PRIFLY, the Navigation Bridge, the deck crews, and the pilots as they go about their work in a world where there is little margin for error.

So all-pervading is the sense of being on board an actual carrier in the Sea-Air Operations gallery that one feels somewhat disoriented and stunned upon emerging from the hangar deck and reentering the Museum to find oneself on land.

March 16th. At sea.
Babe Herman comes on the squawk-box: "Now, Sullivan, bos'n's mate thoid class, foist division, dial zero—belay that woid!" A long pause, then another whistle, and "Sullivan, bos'n's mate *foist* class, *thoid* division, dial 760!"

They say that smell is the strongest stimulus to memory, but if I ever wanted to recreate shipboard life, I'd be hard put to find a scent that would summon it. Except for coffee and burnt powder, I don't believe a warship has any characteristic smell.

I could do it by sounds, though. There are a dozen to choose from, any one of which would make the *Yorktown* or the *Lexington* take shape before my mind's eye: the irregular rattle of the shutter on a blinker; the ticking of a 40mm director, and the clamor of the 40s themselves, like a regiment of recruits trying to keep step up an iron stairway; the muffled roar of the blowers; the clank of a tool dropped on a metal deck; the riveting hammer of the water taps; the grinding SLAM! of the catapult; the soft iambic *pop* of the line gun; and the ripple of the barriers going down, exactly like the ripple of reef points as a mainsail comes about.

As for the gong that calls us to General Quarters, if I heard that same tone ten years after the end of the war, I'd automatically grab for a helmet. —*Aircraft Carrier,* by Lt. Cmdr. J. Bryan III

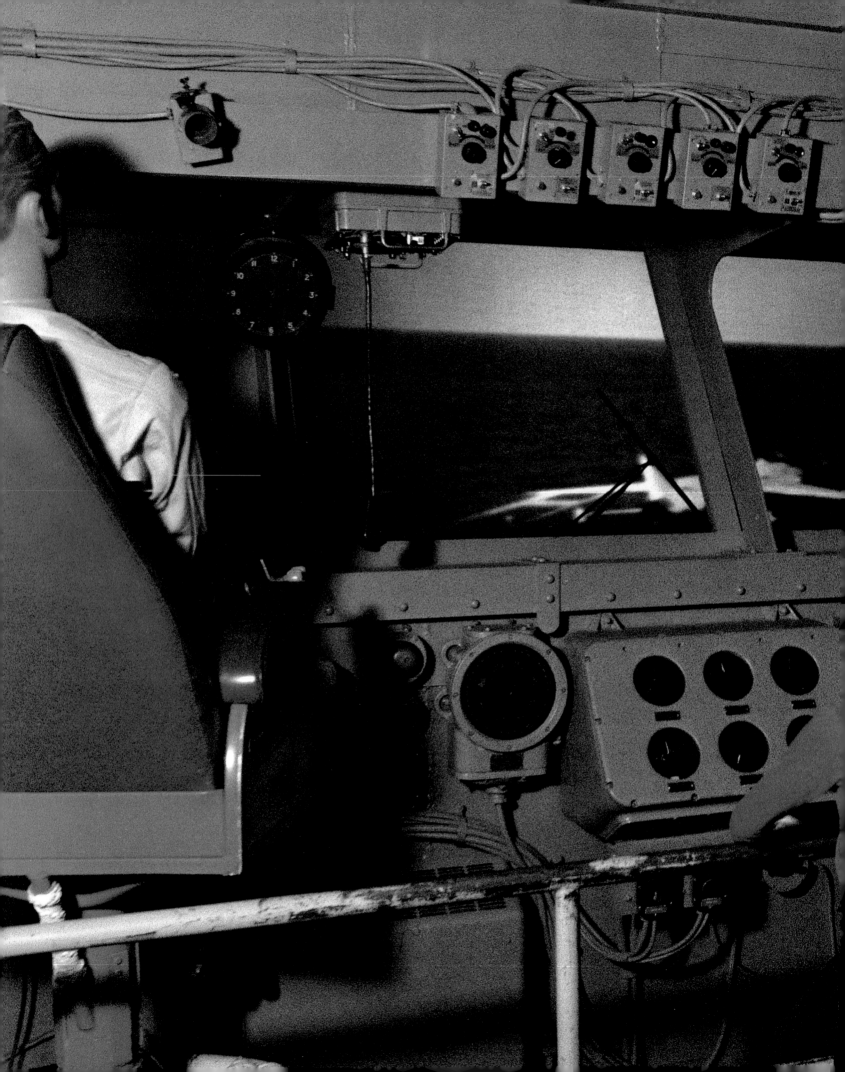

World War II Aviation

Probably no six-year span in the history of aviation saw more astounding advances than the period between 1939 and 1945 during World War II. Biplanes such as the Gloster Gladiator and Fairey Swordfish were operational when the war began; by the war's end, aircraft propelled by jet and rocket engines swept the skies and guided missiles of various types had been employed.

Since the Museum could not possibly show in one gallery more than a very small fraction of the myriad types of aircraft used during World War II, and since none of the 100-foot-plus wingspan multi-engine bombers would fit, the Museum has concentrated on a selection of the best-known fighter aircraft of the major powers—with the exception of Russia. (NASM has no representative Soviet fighter in its collection.) Visitors to the World War II Aviation gallery will find the only Italian Macchi C.202 Folgore (Lightning) known to be on exhibit, an almost equally rare Japanese Mitsubishi A6M5 Zero, Germany's Messerschmitt Bf.109G, Britain's Supermarine Spitfire Mark VII, and America's most outstanding fighter, the North American P-51D Mustang. Representing bombers is the nose section of a twin-engine bomber with one of the most impressive combat records ever achieved by an individual aircraft; it is from the B-26B Marauder *Flak Bait,* which flew 202 combat missions over Germany and German-occupied Holland and France.

Dominating the gallery, however, is Keith Ferris' 25' x 75' mural of the Boeing B-17G *Thunder Bird,* which is so incredibly realistic that the unwary NASM visitor might get the dismaying impression he has entered the World War II Aviation gallery at the precise moment a formation of heavy American bombers has come under attack by German fighters and flak at 25,000 feet.

In "Cowboys and Indians," his fascinating and impressively researched account of the mission depicted by the Ferris mural, Jeff Ethell tells how in March, 1975, NASM's Curator of Art, Jim Dean, telephoned Keith Ferris with the request that he paint a mural showing a formation of B-17 Flying Fortress bombers "representative of the war they fought in." Ferris accepted and asked artist John Clark to be his painting assistant and Ethell to be his researcher. Ferris, Clark, and Ethell agreed to attempt to document a precise moment in history accurate down to the last detail. They first drew up a list of requirements for the aircraft to be depicted: (1) a veteran camouflaged B-17G of the Eighth Air Force with much wear evident; (2) photos of the aircraft available for reference; (3) a known battle record; (4) name and nose art in reasonable taste; (5) a good combination of mission tally symbols and markings—air division, wing, group, squadron and tail markings; and (6) the specific mission to be depicted had to meet the following requirements: a) it had to take place between July and December, 1944, the height of Eighth Air Force activity; b) during good weather, when there were c) contrails, d) flak, and e) enemy fighters.

The field of eligible B-17s was initially narrowed down to nine aircraft and eventually to the 303rd Bomb Group's veteran B-17G *Thunder Bird* because of her long mission history, her colorful markings, the availability of photographs, and her condition. "Was she ever beat up!" Ethell recalled. "Patches all over her skin, paint that was bleached badly, entire replacement parts that were natural aluminum standing out against the olive drab. And she was strictly 'GI' having been flown by so many crews." Once the aircraft was selected, Ethell had the chore of going through the records of each of the 116 missions flown by *Thunder Bird* between July and December, 1944. Only one mission fit their requirements: Mission 72, flown August 15, 1944, against the Luftwaffe fighter airfield at Wiesbaden, Germany.

At 11:22 that morning more than thirty-five years ago, the B-17s dropped their bombs and turned back toward their base at Molesworth, England. Although the raid on Wiesbaden is *Thunder Bird*'s seventy-second bombing mission, it is one of her crew's first exposures to combat. They are flying now at 25,000 feet, visibility is between 10 and 15 miles. By 11:45 German anti-aircraft fire is intense, but the flak is inaccurate, bursting behind the bombers and to their left. Three Luftwaffe fighter wings have already scrambled. JG 300, composed of heavily armed Focke-Wulf Fw 190A-8s and Messerschmitt Bf.109Gs, is the primary unit responsible for attacking the bomber formations. JG 300 is led by Major Walter Dahl. His Sturmgruppe—literally, a Storm Group, a large wedge formation used to penetrate the tight bomber formations—has become famous throughout Germany for its pilots' tactic of ramming bombers if necessary to bring them down, then parachuting to safety. Dahl sees that the bombers are without fighter escort and notifies his division, which gives permission to attack.

With Dahl at the point, the German fighters scream in. They sweep through the formation, the heavy cannon in Dahl's Fw 190 rips the wing off a B-17, and as the Fortress tumbles, Dahl sees three chutes open.

Thunder Bird is in the lead section of the 303rd Bomb Group's thirty-nine B-17s when Dahl's fighters strike the lower section.

Pulling back on his stick after his firing run, Unteroffizier Leopold Bigalke in his Bf.109G *White 12* climbs for an attack on the lead section, then banks to sweep across *Thunder Bird*'s right flank toward a B-17 ahead. Lieutenant Klaus Bretschneider in his Fw 190A-8 *Red One* swings in behind Bigalke's Bf.109 and to its left to close in on the B-17 *Bonnie B* just below *Thunder Bird*'s inboard starboard engine. Both fighters are taking advantage of the bomber formation's contrails as they press in for their attacks. This is the precise moment frozen in Keith Ferris' mural.

The B-17 was one of the best-known and most widely used heavy bombers of World War II. As General Carl "Tooey" Spaatz, the Air Force's first Chief of Staff, told wartime Chief of the United States Army Air Forces General "Hap" Arnold, "The B-17 was the single weapon most responsible for the defeat of Germany." More than 12,700 B-17s were produced by Boeing. Armed with thirteen .50-caliber machine guns including those in its chin, nose, top, and belly (ball) turrets, the turbo-supercharged four-engine bomber could carry 6,000 pounds of bombs some 2,000 miles at 30,000 feet. By the end of 1943, B-17Gs such as those in the mural were being used by many units in the European Theater.

Just as the Sea-Air Operations gallery across the way concentrates on the Pacific Theater of operations, the emphasis in the World War II gallery—despite the presence of the Zero suspended from the ceiling—is on the European Theater. No chronological history is attempted, but significant actions involving the various aircraft displayed are highlighted. Near the Spitfire, for example, are Battle of Britain artifacts and photographs.

The World War II gallery is a large, open room designed to provide the visitor with the best possible vantage points from which to view the aircraft. But perhaps the most extraordinary view in this gallery is that from the B-26 Bomber *Flak Bait*'s forward section.

There may not be a more fitting name for an airplane than the one given this particular bomber; during its 21 months of combat *Flak Bait* collected over 1,000 enemy hits.

The Martin B-26B Marauder started its career with the worst possible reputation. It was a very hot airplane, and its comparatively short wings necessitated high speed, power-on landings, and dangerously high stalling speeds. Due to pilot inexperience, engine failures, runaway propellers, structural weakness in its tail, and so on, there were so many training accidents that Marauders were nicknamed "One-a-Day-in-Tampa Bay," "widow-makers," and, since the wings provided no visible means of support, "The Baltimore Whore." Because of the large number of accidents, on at least four occasions production nearly ceased while Congressional committees—including one headed by then-Missouri Senator Harry S Truman—investigated its design. And yet it was a beautiful machine with symmetrical curves and extremely clean lines. General Jimmy Doolittle was such an outspoken supporter of the Marauder that he flew the aircraft on one engine at training bases around the country to prove to young pilots that any emergency could be safely handled in that plane. But its reputation took a long time to improve, and no amount of training or time could prevent the apparent affinity *Flak Bait* had for attracting bits of enemy metal.

Jim Farrell, *Flak Bait's* pilot, recalled, "It was hit plenty of times—*all* the time. I guess it was hit more than any other plane in the Group." Other aircraft in the 322nd Bomb Group could return from a mission unscathed; *Flak Bait* would come back peppered. The first time B-26s were used in the European Theater was on May 14, 1943, against a power plant in IJmuiden, Holland. Twelve B-26s from the 322nd Bomb Group took part; one plane was lost, every plane was hit—one returned with more than 300 holes. Their target was little damaged. Another mission against IJmuiden was scheduled for three days later. On May 17th, eleven B-26s took off; one was forced to turn back before reaching the Dutch coast. Not one of the remaining ten returned. The raid was a disaster. Every operational B-26, sixty men, and the unit's commanding officer were lost.

"Right after we lost the ten planes at IJmuiden,"* Farrell recalled, "morale was devastated because we had no idea that we weren't going to have every raid just like that—all out, none back. So fellows would take every bit of money they had, go on leave and spend every nickle of it because they didn't think they would be around tomorrow.

---

* Jay P. Spenser, "Flak Bait!", *Airpower Magazine*, vol. 8, no. 5, Sept., 1978.

Others tried to get transferred to the [heavy bombers] and used every bit of influence they had."

The heavy losses were due to an almost criminal misunderstanding of how best to tactically use this superb medium bomber. Marauders could carry 3,000 pounds of bombs, half the load carried by a B-17, but because they lacked superchargers they could not operate at the high altitudes the heavy bombers regularly used above the worst of the flak. Eighth Air Force therefore chose the opposite extreme: B-26s were sent in hedge-hopping 200+ mph, and German defenses were simply too good. Light flak, machine gun, and even small-arms fire came at them from all sides. After the terrible losses at IJmuiden, tactics were changed. Crews were trained in flying tight, high formations where, even though there was more flak, there was less smaller arms fire. "All the airplanes came back pretty well shot up," Farrell said, "a few wounded, but no losses."

After Farrell and his crew had flown their un-named B-26 for several missions they decided they'd have to christen it somehow. Farrell's brother's dog was nicknamed "Flea Bait" and from there to "Flak Bait" was but a short, imaginative hop. As soon as the name was painted on her nose, *Flak Bait* began to receive hits. On September 6, 1943, a Bf.109 took *Flak Bait* on with a head-on pass. A 20mm shell smashed through the B-26's Plexiglas nose and exploded behind the left instrument panel. Miraculously, neither Farrell, nor his co-pilot, Thomas Owen Moore, nor his bombardier/navigator/nose gunner, O. J. "Red" Redmond, was severely wounded. On another mission, a week later, *Flak Bait* returned with a huge chunk taken out of her horizontal stabilizer. Soon after, Don Tyler's tail gun position was hit and the sheet of fuselage metal with his name on it was blown away. Tyler evened the score.

"We were in the 'tail-end-Charlie' position in the low flight," Tyler remembered. "The attack came from about eleven o'clock high and in a shallow dive. The boss only had time to say 'Here they come.' A head-on attack only lasts seconds because the relative

The forward fuselage of the famed B-26B Marauder Flak Bait proudly wears its symbols for 202 bombing missions, 5 decoy missions, and tail-gunner Don Tyler's confirmed kill. This American medium bomber flew more combat missions than any other American bomber and while earning her name, endured 21 months of combat, and suffered more than one thousand enemy hits.

Flak Bait *crew was Lt. Jim Farrell, pilot;
Lt. Thomas F. Moore, co-pilot; Lt. Owen
J. Redmond, bombardier/navigator/nose-
gunner; Sgt. J. D. Thielan, top turret gunner/
armorer; Sgt. Donald Tyler, flight engineer/
tail-gunner; and Sgt. Joseph B. Manuel,
radio operator/waist gunner, whose position
is depicted on the following page.*

speed is so great. But from that angle of attack the Bf.109 was right in my field of fire. My last glimpse of him was he went into a steeper dive and veered left. There were several enemy fighters in the air and you didn't have time to watch anything that was out of your field of fire." A Spitfire pilot observed the enemy crash; confirmation subsequently came through channels.

By October, 1943, six months after the disastrous IJmuiden raids, the morale of the B-26 pilots was high. The Marauders were achieving a bombing accuracy unequaled by any other aircraft and, although the planes were still taking heavy punishment, the losses were astonishingly low. Farrell explains,

Our strong points were our speed and our heavy armament . . . . We had the advantage over the heavies because we were moving much faster than they were in relation to the German fighters. We had many encounters with them early in the war and my feeling is we became too tough for them. For the most part the fighters left us alone and the Germans came at us with flak. Because of our altitude it was more effective with us than it would ever be with the heavies. They were at twenty-seven to thirty thousand feet and we were down at twelve and thirteen thousand feet, but they had to fly pretty much straight and level while we had the advantage of being able to maneuver as a group . . . .

We figured it took the flak guns seventeen seconds to target us and another thirteen before the shells started bursting. For that reason, we wouldn't go thirty seconds without doing something—climbing and turning to the right, descending and turning to the left, etc . . . . There was armor plating bolted to the fuselage on the pilot's side and he had an armor shell behind his seat. I wore a flak vest— it was like an apron—and had the instrument panel in front of me. It was thick enough to stop that 20mm [cannon shell] which is good enough for me.

Flak Bait's *cockpit frames an apparent confrontation between the Museum's Macchi C.202 Folgore and the B-17G Thunder Bird.*

A B-26 co-pilot, however, was not so well protected. The instrument panel was open on his side and the rudder pedals folded back so that the navigator/bombardier could crawl through to the nose. On March 26, 1944, more than 350 B-26 Marauders returned to IJmuiden, Holland, and had their revenge: they dropped over 700 tons of bombs on a Nazi torpedo boat and submarine pens, and only one B-26 was lost.

The B-26 Marauder *Flak Bait* flew its 202nd and final mission in May, 1945. Among its missions were 31 against Pas de Calais V-1 rocket-launching sites, 5 against shipyards and E-boat pens, 45 against railway marshaling yards and communications centers, 35 against German airfields, 31 against Seine River and other bridges, 15 against fuel dumps, 30 against defended towns and cities, and 8 against gun emplacements. She logged 725 hours combat time, dropped over 375,000 pounds of bombs, and flew approximately 178,000 miles.

That fighter plane one can see cutting across *Flak Bait's* nose on its way to Keith Ferris' bomber formation is the Macchi C.202 Folgore, one of the best fighter planes made in the early stages of the war and certainly the best Italian fighter to have been produced in quantity. But despite its high reputation in Italy, it never became as famous as other nations' fighter aircraft even though when the Folgore (Lightning) entered battle in North Africa in the summer of 1941 against the British, in the hands of a skilled pilot, this new machine was more than a match for its adversaries. The Folgore was superbly maneuverable and light-fingered to handle. The Folgore's major drawback was its light armament compared to other fighters. A Spitfire, for example, carried two 20mm and four .303-caliber machine guns; the Folgore mounted only two 12.7mm and two 7.7mm machine guns. After the Italian Armistice in September, 1943, a number of Folgores were flown against the Germans by the small Italian Co-belligerent Air Force.

The Macchi C.202 Folgore suspended from this gallery's ceiling is perhaps the sole remaining aircraft of this type anywhere in the world. A curious, but hardly noticeable facet is that the Folgore's left wing is 8⅜ inches longer than its right, making it one of the rare aircraft to have used this asymmetrical method of counteracting its engine's rotational torque to assist pilot control.

Not many people know that the P-51 Mustang, which many consider the best fighter plane of World War II, was originally built for the British, who had approached North American early in 1940 requesting a quantity of P-40s to alleviate the RAF fighter shortage. North American proposed instead to build an entirely new and superior plane. The British agreed, and were astonished at the speed with which the plane was built at the West Coast manufacturer's plant. By the summer of 1942 the first Mustangs were in combat and the British pilots' enthusiasm was soon obvious. The United States Army Air Forces, however, were still cool to the P-51, regarding it a "foreign" design, and were concentrating on perfecting their Lockheed P-38 Lightnings and Republic P-47 Thunderbolts. But as the Mustang began to prove itself in combat, the USAAF took a closer look. When the P-51's Allison engines were replaced by Rolls-Royce Merlins with two-speed blowers, and the three-bladed propellers were exchanged for four-bladed props, there was no better fighter performing in the air.

That Japanese Mitsubishi A6M5 Zero, which appears to be clawing for air after strafing the Sea-Air Operations gallery's *USS Smithsonian* across the hall, was, to the dismay of Allied pilots who were astounded by its exceptional maneuverability and speed, the primary Japanese Naval fighter throughout World War II. When aircraft carriers were no longer available to the Japanese, the Zero (properly code-named Zeke) was shifted to land bases. Only when the Grumman F6F Hellcat and the North American Mustang reached the Pacific in quantity was the Zero's relative superiority diminished.

A captured Zero undergoing evaluation tests. Note the American star within the rising-sun fuselage insignia.

Divided by floor space in this gallery, as the English Channel separated them during World War II, are two of the Battle of Britain's legendary adversaries: Britain's Supermarine Spitfire Mark VII and Germany's Messerschmitt Bf.109G-6. The Spitfire, though slightly faster and considerably more maneuverable than the thinner and smaller-winged Bf.109, could not match the German plane at higher altitudes, and until the Spit's engine was modified, British pilots often lost their opponent through his dives. But the British had the advantage of fighting over their home island, whereas the German fighter's critical range limited his time over Britain to less than twenty minutes. The Messerschmitt Bf.109E was already in mass production when Germany went to war in 1939, and over a thousand 109s were with operational fighter units. Only 400 Spitfires

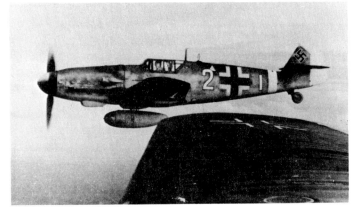

The actual aircraft after which the National Air and Space Museum patterned the markings and camouflage for its Messerschmitt Bf.109G.

were in service. Both aircraft went through various modifications to improve performance. NASM's Spitfire has the extended wingtips of the high-altitude version and its Bf.109 is of the "G" (for "Gustav") series which had two MG-151 wing-mounted 20-mm machine guns, two MG-131 20-mm machine guns mounted in the fuselage and one 30-mm MK-108 cannon firing through its spinner. This armament was ideally suited for bomber interception, but the added weight and drag reduced the 109's efficiency against other fighters.

The Norden Bombsight, one of America's most closely guarded secrets during World War II, is also on exhibit in this gallery. The Norden was a key to the USAAF's daylight high-precision bombing strategy, since only with an extremely accurate bombsight could small military targets be hit from high altitudes. The bombardier set altitude, airspeed, and other factors into his Norden Bombsight (which was basically an automatic speed and distance calculator) and then kept his telescopic viewer's crosshairs centered on his target. As the aircraft moved, ground speed and wind drift were fed into the computer. A bombardier then connected the bombsight to the autopilot, which kept the aircraft on course and released the bombs at the proper time.

Perhaps the one exhibit that will bring a smile to the gallery visitor is the "50-Mission Cap" resting on a silk scarf and a pillow in a glass case. The 50-mission cap was the symbol of an Army Air Force flight crew member with many combat-mission hours behind him. The look of a veteran was achieved by removing the stiffening grommet from the standard service cap so that a radio headset could be worn. With each successive mission the cap would then achieve a more and more pronounced crushed appearance.

That white parachute-silk scarf, typical of those wrapped about fighter pilots' necks, was not just worn as an affectation, or even for warmth. The silk kept the pilot's neck from chafing as he swiveled his head back and forth in search of enemy aircraft.

133

The Museum's P-51 D Mustang, considered by many to be the finest fighter plane of World War II, wears the yellow and black checkerboard colors of the 351st Fighter Squadron, 353rd Fighter Group, Eighth Air Force. This unit, stationed at Raydon, Suffolk, England, was assigned to escort bombers such as Thunder Bird on missions deep into Germany.

The Mustang's cockpit.

The two major British fighters of the Battle of Britain were the Hawker Hurricane (left) and the Supermarine Spitfire (below).

The Spitfire's cockpit.

Early reports of the Japanese Zero's speed, maneuverability, firepower, and range were so incredible that they were rejected as incorrect and unbelievable by American aeronautical experts. Pearl Harbor and the appearance of the Zero in seemingly countless numbers throughout the Pacific in the opening days of the war proved the validity of those reports. The Museum's Mitsubishi Zero Fighter, Model 52 (code named Zeke by the Allies), is presumed to have been one of 12 late-model Zeroes captured on Saipan Island in April, 1944, and sent to the United States for evaluation.

A head-on view of the German Messerschmitt Bf.109G reveals its two MG 131 machine guns and single 30mm MK 108 cannon which fired through the spinner. Although slightly slower and less maneuverable than its first major opponent, the Spitfire, the Bf.109's performance was superior at high altitudes. The Museum's specimen wears the markings and camouflage of ship number 2, 7th Squadron, 3rd Group, 27th Wing that operated in the Eastern Mediterranean during late 1943.

Painstakingly rebuilt at the Garber Facility, the Me 262 seems ready to leap into the sky.

The Messerschmitt ME 262 was faster than any propeller-driven fighter and carried a powerful armament. Some 1,400 were produced by Germany late in World War Two, but only about 300 were actually operational. The rest were either destroyed by bombing or grounded because of shortages.

General Aviation

The theme of the General Aviation gallery is: almost everyone can learn to fly. The films, the planes on display, and other exhibits are present to provide the NASM visitor with an idea of what being a private pilot means.

Today there are more than 200,000 aircraft in use in general aviation and some 744,000 pilots licensed to fly them. "General aviation" encompasses everything except military aviation and scheduled commercial airlines. Sports flying accounts for only 5 percent of general aviation; the overwhelming majority consists of business flights, commuter and air taxi service, instructional and rental use, flights for surveying, agricultural use, and even towing advertising banners. Almost 250,000 people are employed in general aviation—a business that now contributes more than five billion dollars annually to the Gross National Product.

The only aircraft in the Museum that might rank in terms of impact upon the general public with the Hall of Air Transportation's DC-3 is Mr. Piper's little "Cub," which has been called the Model T of aviation. It is the airplane in which thousands of today's general aviation pilots made their first solo and dual instruction flights and for which countless other thousands as youngsters saved up their allowances and chore money for the unforgettable experience of climbing into its noisy, drafty, and cramped cockpit to take their first airplane ride.

The other three aircraft on display in this gallery are a Cessna 180, a Beechcraft Bonanza, and a Gates Learjet 23. The Learjet was the first jet aircraft designed and produced specifically for business and corporate use. Introduced in 1963 and patterned after the Swiss P-16 fighter-bomber, the Learjet is an exceptionally handsome airplane with clean aerodynamic lines offering high speed (561 mph at 24,000 feet), exceptional climbing performance (it can reach 35,000 feet in less than 10 minutes; it holds numerous world performance records for business jets), and demonstrably long range and endurance.

Almost every Museum visitor has heard of Amelia Earhart, but how many of them are familiar with a diminutive Columbus, Ohio, housewife named Geraldine L. Mock? And yet, in this gallery's little Cessna 180 with *Spirit of Columbus* painted on its nose, Geraldine "Jerrie" Mock became the first woman to pilot an aircraft solo around the world, thereby symbolically completing Amelia Earhart's flight. At 9:31 A.M. on March 19, 1964, Mrs. Mock took off from the Columbus, Ohio airport and arrived back home on April 17, having flown 23,103 miles in 29 days, 11 hours, and 59 minutes. On the way, Mrs. Mock set an around-the-world speed record for aircraft weighing less than 3,858 pounds. On May 4, 1964, then-President Lyndon B. Johnson awarded Mrs. Mock for her achievement the Federal Aviation Administration's Gold Medal for Exceptional Service.

The Cessna 180 that Mrs. Mock flew was built in 1953 and passed through several owners, who put 990 flying hours on it before Mrs. Mock bought the plane in 1964. She had additional custom-built fuel tanks fitted inside the cabin and spaces for personal equipment and survival gear installed on board prior to her departure. Upon completing the flight, Mrs. Mock never flew the *Spirit of Columbus* again. Cessna exchanged aircraft with her and gave her a later model.

The Cessna Model 180 was developed early in the 1950s as a rugged four-place light aircraft. Variations on its design have made it popular as a "bush" aircraft in many of the underdeveloped parts of the world.

The Beech Bonanza on exhibit in this gallery carries different markings on the left and right sides of its fuselage in recognition of its two significant flights. The "Waikiki Beech" markings on the Bonanza's left side honor the cross-country record-breaking flight William P. Odom made in this plane on March 6, 7, and 8, 1949 when he flew from Honolulu, Hawaii, to Teterboro, N.J., in 36 hours, 1 minute, thereby establishing an international light-plane distance record of 4,957 Great Circle miles.

Ralph Goings. Fly *with Patco. 1973. Oil on canvas, 36 x 52". From the Stuart M. Speiser Collection*

The sleek Gates Learjet 23.

was reasonably priced, simple to maintain, and easy to fly, it became one of the most popular airplanes in the history of aviation. During World War II the Cub, known as the "Grasshopper," saw extensive service as a trainer, artillery spotter, transport, ambulance, and reconnaissance aircraft. Some 5,673 were delivered to the military during the war.

The other two aircraft on display in this gallery are a Cessna 180 and a Gates Learjet 23. The Learjet was the first jet aircraft designed and produced specifically for business and corporate use. Introduced in 1963 and patterned after the Swiss P-16 fighter-bomber, the Learjet is an exceptionally handsome airplane with clean aerodynamic lines offering high speed (561 mph at 24,000 feet), exceptional climbing performance (it can reach 35,000 feet in less than 10 minutes; it holds numerous world performance records for business jets), and demonstrably long range and endurance. In 1976, golfer Arnold Palmer captained a Learjet 36 which flew around the world in an elapsed time of 57 hours and 26 minutes.

The Cessna 180 Spirit of Columbus *in which, in 1964, "Jerrie" Mock became the first woman to pilot an aircraft solo around the world.*

145

Earlier, in this same aircraft, on January 12, 1949, Odom had established a light-plane record from Hawaii to the U.S. mainland. Both of these flights were sponsored by the Beech Aircraft Corp. to demonstrate the Bonanza which had begun in production two years before. More than 11,000 of these distinctive V-tail Model 35 Bonanzas have been produced. "Waikiki Beech" was the fourth Bonanza built.

After a nationwide tour with the airplane, Odom presented the "Waikiki Beech" to the Smithsonian. In 1951, the Bonanza was returned to Beech to be used by Congressman Peter F. Mack Jr., for an around-the-world goodwill flight. Rechristened "Friendship Flame" the Bonanza with Congressman Mack at the controls took off on October 7, 1951 for a 33,000-mile tour of 45 major cities in 35 countries. The aircraft carries its "Friendship Flame" markings on the right side of its fuselage.

In 1975 Beech Aircraft Corp. refurbished the aircraft for exhibit in the National Air and Space Museum. The only modifications made to this otherwise standard Model 35 Beech Bonanza was the extra 126-gallon fuel tank in its cabin and streamlined 62-gallon fuel tank on each wing tip.

Although the theme of the General Aviation gallery is that almost everyone can fly, the gallery also makes it clear that there is an unspoken but fully understood "yes, but," because obtaining a pilot's certificate is considerably more difficult than getting a license to drive a car. Why?

You have to be able to pass a physical examination. You have to be able to devote the time to study in a ground school where you must master a variety of subjects related to the safe operation of an airplane. These courses, covering the principles of flight, flight instruments, navigation, meteorology, Federal Aviation Administration regulations, and others, take nine weeks, at the end of which one has to pass the rigid FAA exam—which can take as long as four hours. You have to have at least twenty hours of dual instruction and twenty hours of supervised solo flying time, and before you can take your flight check you must pass another oral exam. During your flight check you must demonstrate absolute mastery of the aircraft under all conditions. Flying is not like driving a car. And if you're the sort of person who gets upset over obeying a 55-mph speed limit on the turnpike, then you're not going to be happy flying in an FAA environment. You have to have the sense of responsibility to accept the regulations of the FAA system and to operate within their constraints. You have to know your airplane, your instruments, the mechanics and principles of flight. Flying may be fun, but it's also very serious business.

The general aviation business today is booming. One attraction is that a small private plane can get about 16 miles to the gallon and cover between 120 and 160 miles per hour without being regulated by the road. Yes, everyone can fly, and if you have ever tried to get in or out of Chicago's O'Hare Airport during a holiday weekend, you will have the impression that everyone is.

Science,
Technology,
and the Arts

"To Fly"
NASM's first spectacular film shown in the Museum's IMAX theater on a movie screen five stories high and seven stories wide, quite literally overwhelms each visitor who watches it. Photographed on IMAX (a very large film format nine times the size of a standard movie frame and printed horizontally on 70mm film) and accompanied by an original score composed by the Brazilian concert pianist Bernardo Segall and recorded by a fifty-piece symphony orchestra (with six-track stereo sound that booms out from eleven speakers strategically placed throughout the auditorium), "To Fly" is a half-hour breathtaking visual and auditory cinematic experience that takes the viewer on a flying tour of America from 1831 to, well, 2002.

"To Fly" opens with a balloon ascension in post-Colonial times and the balloonist's near-collision with a church steeple. This bird's eye view of America includes the sensation of barnstorming in an early biplane over California—during which the viewers cling white-knuckled to the armrests of their theater seats as the biplane flips upside down—piloting one of the jets of the Navy's crack Blue Angel acrobatic team as it screams across Arizona's deserts, hang-gliding over California's sea-cliffs, and finally free-floating with a mission to outer space.

Because of the great bulk of the IMAX 70 mm camera, Greg MacGillivray and James Freeman, who co-directed and co-photographed "To Fly," had to design special camera mounts for the helicopter, the Boeing 747 Jumbo Jet, and the RF-4 reconnaissance jet used in filming the aerial sequences. As critical and difficult as these airborne camera scenes were, they could have been reshot if something had gone wrong. The most critical shot, however, was one taken from the ground: the lift-off of the towering Saturn launch vehicle. The launch shown was that of the Saturn which boosted the Apollo crew into orbit in July, 1975, for their link-up with the Soviet Soyuz spacecraft during the Apollo-Soyuz Test Project. If MacGillivray and Freeman had missed that shot it would have been impossible to reshoot; that was the last Saturn launched.

"To Fly" was produced by the Academy Award-winning Francis Thompson, funded by Conoco Inc.

The Museum's second feature film, equally as spectacular as "To Fly," is "Living Planet," also produced by Francis Thompson and funded by Johnson Wax. Here viewers are carried on an aerial journey over many of the Earth's most remote corners—Africa, India, and the Arctic.

The Paul E. Garber Preservation, Restoration and Storage Facility
The Garber Facility (formerly called Silver Hill) is a 24-building complex now open to the public as a "no frills" museum, offering visitors more than one hundred aircraft, spacecraft, power plants, and related objects from the reserve collection of the Museum. Both military and civil aircraft are simply displayed with brief identification labels. Trained guides conduct free tours of the warehouse/exhibition areas, and visitors can enter the restoration area where the technicians can be seen at work preserving aircraft.

The Garber Facility's aircraft conservators are such demanding craftsmen that, at times, they have to be restrained from restoring aircraft to better shape than they were in when they were first built. Air frames are brought back to flight status, engines are not—they are, however, brought to the point where they *could* become operable. But the facility's philosophy is that it is better to spend the time and the money to arrest corrosion in a dozen airplanes than to spend them bringing just one aircraft all the way up to flight status. Still, about twenty artifacts (including propellers, landing gears, and engines) are preserved each year and about four aircraft restored.

One of the major problems facing the craftsmen is that many of the airplanes needing restoration are military. Military aircraft were mass-produced as part of the war effort and were expected to pass inspection, but not to last for an eternity. Their average life expectancy was about ninety days. A good example is the recently restored Messerschmitt Me 262, the world's first operational jet fighter. It was manufactured by the Germans during the latter stages of World War II and although some 1,400 were made, only about 350 were ever flown in combat due to the fuel shortage in 1944.

In order to stop the corrosion process, the Me 262 was completely taken apart, cleaned, then reassembled. The work was doubly difficult because German manufacturers used composite construction techniques combining aluminum with steel in the fighters. One visitor was particularly impressed by the resulting restoration; he had been an engineer in Germany who had worked on the development of the original Me 262. One interesting fact he pointed out was that the Me 262's swept-back wing was not for higher speed as one might have thought but rather to shift the center of gravity.

Visitors to the Garber Facility tend to be either aviation buffs or persons with some direct relationship to a particular aircraft they have come to see. One such was Don Berlin who designed the famous Curtiss P-40. He had been project engineer on the Gamma and went out to Silver Hill with Walter Boyne, NASM Assistant Director and former head of the Garber Facility. Berlin had not seen the Gamma for about forty years, and, as he stood looking at the silver plane with the slight crumple aft of the engine nacelle which had been caused by a particularly hard landing in the Antarctic, he turned to Boyne and said, "I knew it was going to happen. I *knew* what should have been done to strengthen that structure!" And Berlin, according to Boyne, was ready to redraw the aircraft's design.

Among the aircraft stored at the Garber Facility is one that holds an awesome role in the history of military aviation. It is the *Enola Gay*, the B-29 that dropped the atomic bomb on Hiroshima.

Art Gallery

The first works of space art created in strict accord with existing scientific knowledge were the illustrations published in Jules Verne's 1865 novel *From the Earth to the Moon*. Not quite one hundred years later, in 1963, the National Aeronautics and Space Administration, in cooperation with the National Gallery of Art, invited some of this country's foremost artists to contribute their imagination, perceptions, and talent to document the space program in the most ambitious art project since the Works Progress Administration (W.P.A.) artists' projects of the Depression. Much of this resulting art, which transformed space hardware into visions of fantasy and beauty, is in the Museum's Art Gallery, but NASM's art collection is so extensive that paintings, prints, and other works of art overflow the gallery and can be found in almost every exhibit area, office, hallway, and corner of the Museum.

On June 27, 1976, after the Museum opened to the public, *Washington Post* art critic, Wolf Von Eckhart, wrote,

> . . . the Art Gallery, directed by curator James D. Dean, which displays 200 paintings and other artworks, is architecturally and artistically among the most inspired art galleries in Washington. Although everything here is obviously "modern," the art is not confined to one school or *Weltanschauung*. From Rauschenberg to Norman Rockwell, the collection shows us the richness of contemporary creativity.
>
> Nor is the art confined to this gallery. Surprisingly, perhaps, the entire museum is a work of art—a work of art apt to restore one's faith in our time.

The Smithsonian Institution, the parent of the National Air and Space Museum, has a long history of support of, and participation in, scientific studies. In the earliest days of flight, it financed Professor Langley's experiments. Later a grant from the Smithsonian aided Robert Goddard in the development of his rocket designs.

Today research at the Museum continues

The Center for Earth and Planetary Studies, established in 1973, is one of the National Air and Space Museum's scientific research arms. Among the Center's research sources is a complete collection of over 60,000 lunar and planetary photographs taken both by the Apollo astronauts and unmanned probes. Under the direction of Farouk El-Baz, the Center staff works on the mapping and naming of lunar features and on the interpretation of the geologic history of the Moon and planets. The Center also works with NASA on the planning of lunar cartographic projects.

Research on Earth-related subjects has included analysis of data from the July 1975 Apollo-Soyuz Test Project. The Center's automated videodisc library of planetary images provides the basis for continuing comparative planetology studies.

Research efforts are also a major activity of two other departments at the National Air and Space Museum: Space Science and Exploration, and Aeronautics.

Historical research is a prime interest of the Aeronautics Department, directed by Donald S. Lopez. A multi-volume history of aviation is in process. This scholarly publication will cover man's earliest attempts at flight through the jet age. Curators are also at work documenting the history of women in aviation in the United States.

The primary focus of the Space Science and Exploration Department, created in 1980, is also historical research. Under the direction of Paul A. Hanle, department projects include interviewing pioneers in space exploration, preserving their recollections for future use by scholars;

examining closely the beginnings and development of the Space Telescope (to be launched by NASA in 1985) as well as the policy decisions that determine its ultimate design. A history of the Space Telescope is in preparation in cooperation with Johns Hopkins University.

Both departments also provide a range of public services that include traveling exhibits, publications, lectures and films.

The National Air and Space Museum Branch Library is part of the system of Smithsonian Institution Libraries that supports the research and exhibit programs of the Institution and the specialized interests of the staff and the public it serves. It works in conjunction with NASM's collection management staff. The NASM collection contains over 30,000 books, 5,000 bound periodicals, and 500,000 technical reports, and its unrivaled documentary archival collection includes more than one million photographs and other materials covering the history of aviation and space, flight and lighter-than-air technology, the aerospace industry and biography, rocketry, earth and planetary sciences, and astronomy. The rare and scarce aeronautica and astronautica of the Museum are housed in the Admiral DeWitt Clinton Ramsey Room. There one finds over 1,500 pieces of aeronautical sheet music in the Bella Landauer collection in addition to the William A. M. Burden collection of early ballooning works. The NASM archival team is doing pioneering work with both microfiche and videodisc technology to assist in the preservation and dissemination of this material.

Aviation Chronology

November 21, 1783: The first flight in history is made by de Rozier and d'Arlandes in a Montgolfier hot-air balloon at Paris.

December 1, 1783: First flight in a hydrogen balloon (by Charles and Robert) at Paris.

January 7, 1785: Blanchared and Jeffries, in a balloon, make the first Channel crossing by air.

January 9, 1785: Jean Pierre Blanchard makes the first flight in America. Launching his balloon from a Philadelphia prison yard, he flies to Gloucester County, New Jersey.

October 22, 1797: Garnerin, from a balloon, makes the first parachute descent from the air.

1799: Cayley designs first modern configuration airplane, incorporating fixed wings, tail-unit control surfaces, and an auxiliary method of propulsion.

1804: First modern configuration airplane, Cayley's model glider, flies.

1809–10: Cayley publishes his classic triple paper on aviation, which lays the foundations of modern aerodynamics.

1853: First man-carrying flight in a heavier-than-air craft (Cayleys "coachman-carrier" glider)—but not under control by the occupant.

1876: Otto invents the four-stroke petrol engine.

1881-96: Lilienthal's first successful piloted gliding flights.

1889: Lilienthal publishes his classic, *Der Vogelflug als Grundlage der Fliegekunst.*

1896: Langley obtains his first success with two of his steam-powered tandem-wing models.

1899: The Wright Brothers invent a system of wing-warping for control in roll, and fly a kite incorporating it.

1901: The Wrights fly their No. 2 glider near Kitty Hawk.

1902: The Wrights make nearly 1,000 glides on their No. 3 glider and invent coordinated warp and rudder control, i.e., combined control in roll and yaw.

December 17, 1903: The first powered, sustained, and controlled airplane flights in history, by Wilbur and Orville Wright, near Kitty Hawk; the first of four flights lasts for 12 seconds, the last for 59 seconds.

September 20, 1904: First circle flown, by Wilbur Wright; this is witnessed and described by A.I. Root.

June, 1905: First fully practical powered airplane, the Wright Flyer III, flies.

October–November, 1906: Santos-Dumont makes the first official powered hop-flights in Europe; the best (November 12) covers 721 feet in 21⅕ seconds..

August 8, 1908: At Hunaudières, France, Wilbur Wright flies in public for the first time in the first practical two-seat airplane, and transforms aviation by his display of flight controls.

September 3, 1908: Orville Wright first flies in public at Fort Myer, Virginia.

October 30, 1908: Henri Farman completes the first cross-country flight, flying 16½ miles.

July 25, 1909: On his No. XI monoplane, Louis Blériot makes the first Channel crossing from near Calais to Dover.

August, 1909: First great aviation meeting is held at Reims, and has widespread influence, showing the airplane is now a practical vehicle.

February, 1910: Hugo Junkers receives a patent for the design of a cantilever flying wing aircraft.

November 14, 1910: Eugene Ely takes off from the USS *Birmingham* in a Curtiss Pusher—the birth of the aircraft carrier.

January 18, 1911: Eugene Ely lands his Curtiss Pusher aboard the armored cruiser USS *Pennsylvania*, at anchor in San Francisco Bay—the first landing of an airplane on a ship.

1912: Ruchonnet and Bechereau introduce monocoque construction on the record-setting *Monocoque Deperdussin* racer, which wins the Gordon Bennett Cup by setting a world's speed record of 108.18 mph.

The first enclosed cabin airplanes (British Avro) and all-metal airplanes (the *Tubavion* of Ponche and Primard) complete their initial flights.

1913: The first multiengine aircraft having four engines, the Sikorsky Bolshoi, completes its initial flights in Russia.

1915: First flight of the Junkers J 1, the world's first all-metal cantilever monoplane.

May 16–17, 1919: First transatlantic flight via the Azores by the NC-4 flying boat of the United States Navy.

1920: First flight of an airplane having a practical retracting landing gear, the Dayton-Wright R.B. racer. This aircraft also had the first variable-camber wing.

March, 1920: First flight test verification of the advantages of equipping an airplane with wing slots.

September 18, 1921: Lt. John A. Macready exceeds the world altitude record for airplanes by reaching 34,508 feet in a Packard-LePere fighter.

September 4, 1922: First transcontinental flight across the United States in a single day, by Lt. James H. "Jimmy" Doolittle, in a D.H. 4B biplane, from Pablo Beach, Florida, to Rockwell Field, San Diego, a distance of 2,163 miles.

January 9, 1923: First successful flight of the Cierva C.3 Autogiro, at Madrid. The Autogiro subsequently has great influence on the development of other rotary-wing aircraft, especially helicopters.

May 2-3, 1923: First nonstop transcontinental flight across the United States, from New York to San Diego, by Lts. Oakley Kelly and John A. Macready, in the Fokker T-2 monoplane, a distance of 2,520 miles in 26 hours, 50 minutes.

1924: The trimotor airliner (Junkers G.23) and the Fowler wing flap make their first appearance.

April 6–September 29, 1924: Two Douglas World Cruiser aircraft of the United States Army Air Service complete the first round-the-world, first transpacific, and first westbound Atlantic crossing, flying 26,345 miles in a flying time of 363 hours.

May 20–21, 1927: Charles Lindbergh crosses the Atlantic from New York to Paris, the first solo nonstop crossing and the first by a single-engine aircraft.

July 4, 1927: First flight of the Lockheed Vega, a trend-setting cantilever-wing aircraft having a monocoque fuselage with stressed-skin construction, which imparts lighter weight and larger volume to the aircraft, as well as reducing drag and, thus, boosting performance.

September 24, 1929: James H. Doolittle makes the first blind flight in aviation history, flying a specially instrumented Consolidated-Guggenheim NY-2 research airplane.

1930: Frank Whittle takes out his first patents on turbojet engine design.

September 29, 1931: RAF Flight Lt. George Stainforth completes the world's first flight faster than 400 mph in the Supermarine S.6B racing floatplane.

1933: Introduction of the controllable-pitch propeller on regular airline aircraft, beginning with the Boeing 247. This development, the result of work by Frank Caldwell, greatly improves airplane performance at both low and cruising speeds.

February 8, 1933: First flight of an advanced all-metal monoplane transport, the Boeing 247.

July 1, 1933: First flight of the Douglas DC-1, an innovative all-metal monoplane transport that serves as the basis for the future DC-2 and DC-3 series, which dominate American and much foreign air transport services.

July 28, 1934: Balloonists A.W. Stevens, W.E. Kepner, and O.A. Anderson reach an altitude of 60,613 feet aboard the National Geographic Society—Air Corps balloon *Explorer I.*

September 13, 1935: Howard Hughes sets an international speed record for landplanes, by flying more than 352 mph over a special 3-kilometer course at Santa Ana, California, in the Hughes American Racer, subsequently designated the H-1.

November 11, 1935: Balloonists O.A. Anderson and A.W. Stevens reach a world altitude record for manned balloons of 72,395 feet, in the balloon *Explorer II.*

June 26, 1936: First flight of the world's first practical helicopter, the double-rotor Focke-Achgelis FW-61.

January 20, 1937: Howard Hughes sets a transcontinental nonstop flying time record of 7 hours, 28 minutes, and 25 seconds, in the Hughes H-1 Racer, flying from Burbank, California, to Newark, New Jersey.

1938: The National Advisory Committee for Aeronautics develops a family of low-drag laminar-flow airfoil sections ideally suited for high-speed aircraft designs.

December 31, 1938: First flight of a passenger airplane having a pressurized cabin, the Boeing 307 Stratoliner.

June 30, 1939: First flight of an airplane equipped with a liquid-fuel rocket engine, the Heinkel He-176.

August 27, 1939: Erich Warsitz completes the first jet flight in aviation history, flying the experimental Heinkel He-178, a Von Ohain turbojet.

May 13, 1940: Igor Sikorsky completes the first flight of the Sikorsky VS-300 helicopter, the first successful single-rotor helicopter in the world.

May 15, 1941: First flight of the Gloster E. 28/39, the first British turbojet airplane, powered by a Whittle engine.

February, 1942: First flight of the Douglas DC-4 transport, which sets the future design configuration for postwar four-engine airliners.

October 1, 1942: First flight of the Bell XP-59A Airacomet, the United States' first turbojet aircraft, at Muroc Dry Lake, California.

December, 1943: American military and civilian aeronautical research directors complete initial discussion on using manned research aircraft to fly faster than the speed of sound.

1944: The first turbojet-propelled fighters, the Gloster Meteor and Messerschmitt Me 262, enter service, as does the first operational rocket-propelled interceptor, the Messerschmitt Me 163 *Komet*.

September 20, 1945: The first flight of a turboprop-driven airplane is made in England by a modified Gloster Meteor powered by two Rolls Royce Trent turboprops.

Late 1945: Regularly scheduled commercial aircraft begin transatlantic passenger service.

September 29–October 1, 1946: The Lockheed P2V Neptune *Truculent Turtle* establishes a world's record distance without refueling for 11,235 miles (18,088 kilometers) in 55 hours and 17 minutes.

October 14, 1947: Capt. Charles E. Yeager becomes the first pilot to exceed the speed of sound, flying the air-launched experimental Bell XS-1 rocket-propelled research airplane to Mach 1.06, 700 mph (1,127 kph) at 43,000 feet (13,106.40 meters), over Muroc Dry Lake, California.

April 21, 1949: First flight of a ramjet-powered airplane—the French-built experimental air-launched Leduc 010—which flies for 12 minutes and attains a speed of 450 mph (725 kph) using only half of its available power.

August 25, 1949: First emergency use of a partial-pressure pilot-protection suit, by Maj. Frank K. Everest, on board the Bell X-1, following loss of cabin pressurization at 69,000 feet (21,031 meters).

June 20, 1951: First flight of the Bell X-5 variable-wing-sweep testbed, by Jean Ziegler, at Edwards Air Force Base.

December, 1951: Richard Whitcomb verifies the Area Rule concept to reduce aircraft drag characteristics at transonic and supersonic speeds. This concept, popularized as the so-called "Coke bottle" or "wasp waist" shape, is first verified by flight testing on the Convair F-102.

April 21, 1952: The world's first production turbojet transport, the De Havilland Comet, enters airline service with BOAC.

November 20, 1953: Research test pilot A. Scott Crossfield becomes the first pilot to exceed Mach 2, twice the speed of sound, in an experimental air-launched rocket-propelled Douglas D-558-2 skyrocket. The plane attains Mach 2.005, approximately 1,328 mph (2,138 kph) over Edwards Air Force Base, California.

July 15, 1954: First flight of an American jet transport, the Boeing 707, prototype for the extremely successful Boeing 707 transport and KC-135 transport/tanker aircraft.

November 2, 1954: Flying the propeller-driven Convair XFY-1 Pogo experimental VTOL fighter, test pilot J.F. Coleman completes the first transition from a vertical takeoff to level flight and then back to a vertical descent and landing, at San Diego, California.

September 27, 1956: Capt. Milburn Apt, United States Air Force, becomes the first pilot to fly three times faster than the speed of sound, reaching Mach 3.196, 2,094 mph (3,371 kph) in the Bell X-2. Apt is killed, however, when the plane tumbles out of control into the Mojave Desert.

November 28, 1956: Peter Girand, flying the experimental Ryan X-13 Vertijet VTOL airplane, completes the world's first jet vertical takeoff and transition to level flight.

September 17, 1959: First powered flight of the North American X-15 hypersonic research airplane, by test pilot A. Scott Crossfield, at Edwards Air Force Base, California.

August 16, 1960: Capt. Joseph W. Kittinger, Jr., makes a record parachute descent by jumping from the balloon *Excelsior III* at an altitude of 102,800 feet and free-falling 17 miles before opening his parachute at 17,500 feet.

1961: The North American X-15 research airplane completes the first manned flights of a winged aircraft to Mach 4, 5, and 6.

September 12, 1961: The Hawker P.1127 experimental vectored-thrust research airplane completes its first transition from vertical takeoff to horizontal flight, and back to a vertical landing. The P.1127 serves as the basis for the world's first operational VTOL fighter, the Hawker-Siddeley Harrier.

August 22, 1963: NASA research pilot Joseph Walker attains an altitude of 354,200 feet (67.08 miles) in the hypersonic North American X-15 research airplane, the highest flight to that date by a winged aircraft, at Edwards Air Force Base, California.

September 21, 1964: First flight of the North American XB-70A Mach 3 experimental research airplane. The two XB-70s built furnished much valuable information useful to the design of large supersonic aircraft.

March 7, 1965: A Qantas Airlines' Boeing 707 makes commercial aviation's first nonstop Pacific Ocean crossing, flying from San Francisco to Sydney in 14 hours and 33 minutes.

July 12, 1966: First test flight of the Northrop/NASA M2-F2 lifting-body testbed by Milton O. Thompson, at Edwards Air Force Base, California. The lifting-body concept was being studied as one means of accomplishing manned re-entry from space.

October 3, 1967: Maj. William J. Knight sets a new unofficial world airspeed record for winged aircraft of 4,534 mph (Mach 6.72) in the North American X-15A-2; this is the fastest winged flight and the fastest X-15 flight ever made.

December 31, 1968: First flight of a supersonic transport, the Soviet Tupolev TU-144.

November 24, 1970: First test flight of the NASA supercritical wing, developed by Richard T. Whitcomb, on a North American–Rockwell T-2C trainer.

May 25, 1972: First flight of an aircraft completely dependent on an electronic digital fly-by-wire control system, using a NASA-modified Ling-Temco-Vought F-8 aircraft.

August 23, 1977: Dr. Paul MacCready's *Gossamer Condor*, powered only by the pilot, Bryan Allen, completes a 880-yard figure-8 flight to win the Kremer Prize.

July 12, 1979: The *Gossamer Albatross*, also designed by MacCready and flown by Bryan Allen, completes the first wholly man-powered flight across the English Channel.

Technical Appendix

The technical data presented here apply to the major aircraft and spacecraft appearing in this book. The numbers at the left of each entry refer to the pages on which the vehicle is illustrated.

Milestones of Flight

9, 12–13, 23 WRIGHT 1903 FLYER
Wingspan	12.29m (40 ft. 4 in.)
Length	7.41m (21 ft. ⅜ in.)
Height	2.82m (9 ft. 3¼ in.)
Weight	Empty, 274kg (605 lb.)

16–17 LILIENTHAL STANDARD GLIDER
Wingspan	7.93m (26 ft.)
Wing area	140 sq. ft.
Length	4.19m (13 ft. ¾ in.)
Height	1.53m (5 ft.)
Camber	1-15/1-18

20–21 LANGLEY AERODROME #5 (1896)
Wingspan	4.2m (13 ft. 8 in.)
Length	4.03m (13 ft. 2 in.)
Height	1.25m (4 ft. 1 in.)
Weight	11.25kg (25 lb.)
Engine	Langley, approximately 1 hp

24, 26–27, 30 RYAN NYP SPIRIT OF ST. LOUIS
Wingspan	14.02m (46 ft.)
Length	8.41m (27 ft. 7 in.)
Height	2.99m (9 ft. 10 in.)
Weight	Gross, 2.329kg (5,135 lb.) Empty, 975kg (2,150 lb.)
Engine	Wright Whirlwind J-5-C, 223 hp

Pioneers of Flight

32–33 WRIGHT EX VIN FIZ
Wingspan	9.60m (31 ft. 6½ in.)
Length	6.53m (21 ft. 5 in.)
Height	2.23m (7 ft. 4 in.)
Weight	Gross, 410kg (903 lb.)
Engine	Wright, 35 hp

34–35 FOKKER T-2
Wingspan	24.26m (79.57 ft.)
Length	15.00m (49.20 ft.)
Height	3.71m (12.17 ft.)
Weight	Gross, 4,922kg (10,850 lb.)
Engine	Liberty V-12, 420 hp

38–39 DOUGLAS WORLD CRUISER
Wingspan	15.24m (50 ft.)
Length	20.66m (35 ft. 6 in.)
Height	4.15m (13 ft. 7½ in.)
Weight	Gross, 3,348kg (7,380 lb.), landplane; 3,710kg (8,180 lb.), seaplane Empty, 1,987kg (4,380 lb.), landplane; 2,350kg (5,180 lb.) seaplane
Engine	Liberty V-12, 420 hp

40–41, 48–49 CURTISS R3C-2
Wingspan	Upper, 6.71 (22 ft.) Lower, 6.10m (20 ft.)
Length	6.01m (19 ft. 8½ in.)
Height	2.46m (8 ft. 1 in.)
Weight	Gross, 1,152kg (2,539 lb.) Empty, 975kg (2,150 lb.)
Engine	(1925) Curtiss V-1400, 610 hp; (1926) Curtiss V-1400, 665 hp

42–43 LOCKHEED SIRIUS "TINGMISSARTOQ"
Wingspan	13.05m (42 ft. 10 in.)
Length	9.14m (30 ft.)
Height	4.50m (14 ft. 9 in.)
Weight	Gross, 3,502kg (7,699 lb.) Empty, 2,082kg (4,589 lb.)
Engine	Wright Cyclone SR-1820-F2, 710 hp

44–45 LOCKHEED VEGA
Wingspan	12.49m (41 ft.)
Length	8.38m (27 ft. 6 in.)
Height	2.49m (8 ft. 2 in.)
Weight	Gross, 1,315–1,450kg (2,900–3,200 lb.) Empty, 748kg (1,650 lb.)
Engine	Pratt & Whitney Wasp CB #3812, 225 hp

47 BOEING P-26A
Wingspan	8.52m (27 ft. 11½ in.)
Length	7.26m (23 ft. 10 in.)
Height	3.18m (10 ft. 5 in.)
Weight	Gross, 1,340kg (2,955 lb.) Empty, 996kg (2,196 lb.)
Engine	Pratt & Whitney R-1340-25, 500 hp

50–51 TURNER RT-14 "Meteor"
Wingspan	7.71m (25 ft. 3½ in.)
Length	7.11m (23 ft. 4 in.)
Height	3.05m (10 ft.)
Weight	Gross, 2,233kg (4,923 lb.) Empty, 1,427kg (3,300 lb.)
Engine	Pratt & Whitney Twin Wasp, Sr., 1000 hp.

52–53 BÜCKER 133 JUNGMEISTER
Wingspan	6.60m (21 ft. 7½ in.)
Length	5.90m (19 ft. 4 in.)
Height	2.25m (7 ft. 4½ in.)
Weight	Gross, 585kg (1,290 lb.) Empty, 420kg (925 lb.)
Engine	Warner, 185 hp

Hall of Air Transportation

54–55, 68–69 DOUGLAS DC-3
Wingspan	28.95m (95 ft.)
Length	19.66m (64 ft. 6 in.)
Height	5m (16 ft. 11 in.)
Weight	Gross, 11,430kg (25,200 lb)
Cruising speed	297.65 km/hr (185 mph)
Engine	Two Pratt & Whitney R1830-92, 1,200 hp

58–59 DOUGLAS M-2 MAILPLANE
Wingspan	12.09m (39 ft. 8 in.)
Length	8.81m (28 ft. 11 in.)
Height	3.07m (10 ft. 1 in.)
Weight	Gross, 2,253kg (4,968 lb.) Empty, 1,320kg (2,910 lb.)
Engine	Liberty 12; 400 hp

60–61 PITCAIRN PA-5 MAILWING
Wingspan	10.05m (33 ft.)
Length	6.67m (21 ft. 10½ in.)
Height	2.83m (9 ft. 3½ in.)
Weight	Gross, 1,139kg (2,512 lb.) Empty, 731kg (1,612 lb.)
Engine	Wright Whirlwind J-5-C, 200 hp

63 NORTHROP ALPHA
Wingspan	13m (41 ft. 10 in.)
Length	8.65m (28 ft. 4½ in.)
Height	2.7m (9 ft.)
Weight	Gross, 2,043kg (4,500 lb.) Empty, 1,208kg (2,660 lb.)
Engine	Pratt & Whitney Wasp. 420 hp

64–65 FORD TRI-MOTOR
Wingspan	23.71m (77 ft. 10 in.)
Length	15.18m (49 ft. 10 in.)
Height	4.16m (13 ft. 8 in.)
Weight	Gross, 5,738kg (12,650 lb.) Empty, 3,470kg (7,650 lb.)
Engine	Three Pratt & Whitney Wasp, 420 hp

66–67 BOEING 247D
Wingspan	22.55m (74 ft.)
Length	15.72m (51 ft. 7 in.)
Height	3.70m (12 ft. 1¾ in.)
Weight	Gross, 7,623kg (16,805 lb.)
Engine	Pratt & Whitney Wasp S1H1-G, 550 hp

70 BEECHCRAFT MODEL 18
Wingspan	14.5m (47 ft. 7 in.)
Length	10.4m (33 ft. 11½ in.)
Height	2.8m (9 ft. 2½ in.)
Weight	Gross, 3,967kg (8,750 lb.) Empty, 2,584kg (5,697 lb.)
Engine	Two Pratt & Whitney Wasp, Jr., 450 hp

Balloons and Airships

74–75 *HINDENBURG*
Length	245m (803.8 ft.)
Diameter	41.2m (135.1 ft.)
Height	49.9m (164 ft.)
Volume	199,976 cu m (7,062, 100 cu. ft.)
Engine	Four Daimler-Benz 16-cylinder Diesel, 1,050 hp

World War I Aviation

78–79 SPAD VII
Wingspan	Upper, 7.82m (25 ft. 8 in.) Lower, 7.62m (25 ft.)
Length	6.10m (20 ft.)
Height	3.05m (10 ft.)
Engine	Hispano-Suiza 8Ab. 205 hp

80–81 ALBATROS D. Va
Wingspan	9m (29 ft. 7 in.)
Length	7.33m (24 ft. ⅝ in.)
Height	2.84m (9 ft. 4 in.)
Weight	Gross, 915kg (2,017 lb.) Empty, 680kg (1,499 lb.)
Engine	Mercedes D. IIIa 6-cylinder, in-line water cooled, 180 hp

84–85 SPAD XVI
Wingspan	11.06m (36 ft. 10½ in.)
Length	7.6m (25 ft. 4 in.)
Height	2.525m (8 ft. 5 in.)
Weight	Gross, 1,292.75kg (2,844 lb.) Empty, 906.36kg (1,994 lb.)
Engine	Lorraine-Dietrich Model 8Bb, 250 hp

86–87 FOKKER D. VII
Wingspan	Upper, 8.93m (29 ft. 3½ in.) Lower, 6.86m (22 ft. 10 in.)
Length	7.01m (23 ft.)
Height	2.82m (9 ft. 3 in.)
Weight	Gross, 878kg (1,936 lb.) Empty, 700kg (1,540 lb.)
Engine	Mercedes, 160 hp, or B.M.W., 185 hp

90 SPAD XIII
Wingspan	8m (26.25 ft.)
Length	6.2m (20.35 ft.)
Height	2.52m (8.27 ft.)
Weight	Gross, 924kg (2,036 lb.) Empty, 664kg (1,464 lb.)
Engine	Hispano-Suiza, 220 hp

Flight Technology

91 WESTINGHOUSE YANKEE 9.5A (J-32) ENGINE
Type	Axial-flow turbojet
Diameter	241mm (9.5 in.)
Length	1,402mm (55.2 in.)
Weight	66kg (145 lb.)
Specific fuel consumption	1.7kg/kg t/hr 1.7 lb./lb.t./hr.
Thrust	118kg t (260 lb. t.)

94–95 HUGHES H-1 RACER
Wingspan	9.67m (31 ft. 9 in.)
Length	8.23m (27 ft.)
Weight	Gross, 2.495kg (5,500 lb.)
Engine	Pratt & Whitney Twin Wasp, Jr., 700 hp

Flight Testing

98–99 LOCKHEED VEGA *WINNIE MAE*
Wingspan	12.49m (41 ft.)
Length	8.38m (27 ft. 6 in.)
Height	2.49m (8 ft. 2 in.)
Weight	Gross, 2,041kg (4,500 lb.) Empty, 1,777kg (2,595 lb.)
Engine	Pratt & Whitney Wasp C, serial no. 3088, 500 hp

100–101 HAWKER XV-6A KRESTREL
Wingspan	6.98m (22 ft. 11 in.)
Length	12.93m (42 ft. 5 in.)
Height	3.28m (10 ft. 9 in.)
Weight	Gross, 6,804kg (15,000 lb.) Empty, 4,536kg (10,000 lb.)
Engine	Rolls Royce Bristol Engine Div. Pegasus 5, 15,500-lb. static thrust

102–103 BELL XP-59A AIRACOMET
Wingspan	14.93m (49 ft.)
Length	11.83m (38 ft. 10 in.)
Height	3.76m (12 ft. 3¾ in.)
Weight	Gross, 5,443kg (12,562 lb.) Empty, 3,320kg (7,320 lb.)
Engine	Two General Electric I-A, 1,250-lb. thrust

Vertical Flight

108–109 SIKORSKY XR-4
Rotor Diameter	11.6m (38 ft.)
Length	10.36m (33 ft. 11½ in.)
Height	3.78m (12 ft. 5 in.)
Weight	Gross 1,148kg (2,540 lb.) Empty, 913kg (2,010 lb.)
Engine	Warner R-500-1 Super Scarab, 175 hp

110–111 KELLETT XO-60
Length	Blades folded, 7.90m (25 ft. 11 in.)
Height	3.09m (10 ft. 2 in.)
Weight	Gross, 1,198kg (2,640 lb.)
Engine	Jacobs R-915-3, 300 hp

Sea-Air Operations

116–117 BOEING F4B-4
Wingspan	9.15m (30 ft.)
Length	6.10m (20 ft. 1 in.)
Height	2.84m (9 ft. 4 in.)
Weight	Gross, 1,639kg (3,611 lb.) Empty, 1,069kg (2,354 lb.)
Engine	Pratt & Whitney R-1340-16, 550 hp

118–119 DOUGLAS A-4C SKYHAWK
Wingspan	8.39m (27 ft. 6 in.)
Length	12.23m (40 ft.)
Height	4.58m (15 ft.)
Weight	Gross, 10,215kg (22,500 lb.) Empty, 4,367kg (9,619 lb.)
Engine	Wright J65-W-16A, 3,496kg (7,700 lb.) thrust

World War II Aviation

128–129, 130–131 MARTIN B-26B *FLAK BAIT*
Wingspan	21.63m (71 ft.)
Length	17.76m (58 ft. 3 in.)
Height	6.55m (21 ft. 6 in.)
Weight	Gross, 16,783kg (37,000 lb.) Empty, 10,886kg (24,000 lb.)
Engine	Pratt & Whitney R-2800-43, 1,920 hp

134–135 P-51D MUSTANG
Wingspan	11.28m (37 ft. 5/16 in.)
Length	9.83m (32 ft. 3 in.)
Height	4.16m (13 ft. 8 in.)
Weight	Gross, 5,262kg (11,600 lb.) Empty, 3,232kg (7,125 lb.)
Engine	Rolls-Royce Merlin, 1,695 hp

136 HAWKER HURRICANE 11C (at Silver Hill Museum)
Wingspan	12.2m (40 ft.)
Length	9.8m (32 ft. 2¼ in.)
Height	4.04m (13 ft. 1 in.)
Weight	Gross, 3,445kg (7,544 lb.) Empty, 2,575kg (5,658 lb.)
Engine	Rolls-Royce Merlin XX, 1,260 hp

General Aviation

136–137 SUPERMARINE SPITFIRE

Wingspan	11.05m (36 ft. 10 in.)
Length	8.975m (29 ft. 11 in.)
Height	3.575m (11 ft. 5 in.)
Weight	Gross, 3,575kg (7,875 lb.)
Engine	Rolls-Royce Merlin 64; 1,290 hp at 3,000 rpm

133, 138–139 MITSUBISHI A6M5 ZERO-FIGHTER

Wingspan	11m (36 ft. 1 in.)
Length	9.12m (29 ft. 11 in.)
Height	3.51m (11 ft. 6 in.)
Weight	Gross, 2,733kg (6,025 lb.) Empty, 1,876kg (4,136 lb.)
Engine	NKIF Sakae 21, 1,130 hp

133, 140 MESSERSCHMITT BF. 109G

Wingspan	9.92m (32 ft. 6½ in.)
Length	9.02m (29 ft. 7 in.)
Height	3.40m (11 ft. 2 in.)
Weight	Gross, 3,150kg (6,945 lb.) Empty, 2,700kg (5,953 lb.)
Engine	Daimler-Benz DB605A-ITA, 1,475 hp

141 MESSERSCHMITT Me262

Wingspan	12.48m (40 ft. 11½ in.)
Length	12.13m (39 ft. 9½ in.)
Height	3.84m (12 ft. 7 in.)
Weight	Gross, 6,010kg (13,250 lb.) Empty, 4,419kg (9,742 lb.)
Engines	Junkers Jumo 004B, 898kg (1,980 lb.) static thrust each

144–145 GATES LEARJET 23

Wingspan	10.8m (35 ft. 7 in.)
Length	13.2m (43 ft. 3 in.)
Height	3.8m (12 ft. 7 in.)
Weight	Gross, 5,783kg (12,750 lb.) Empty, 2,790kg (6,150 lb.)
Engine	Two General Electric CJ610-4 turbojets, 1,293kg (2,850 lb.) thrust each

144–145 CESSNA 180 *SPIRIT OF COLUMBUS*

Wingspan	10.97m (36 ft.)
Length	7.98m (26 ft. 2 in.)
Height	2.36m (7 ft. 9 in.)
Weight	Gross, 1,157kg (2,550 lb.)
Engine	Continental O-470-A, 225 hp

Bibliography

Ballantine, Ian, ed., *The Aviation Art of Keith Ferris*, New York, 1978.

Barker, T. Ellis, trans., *Captain Manfred Freiherr Von Richthofen*. New York, 1918.

Boyne, Walter J., "The Gallery of Air Transportation," *Aviation Quarterly*, vol. 2., no. 4, 1976.

———, "Those Anonymous Cubs," *Aviation Quarterly*, vol. 1., no. 4, 1975.

Branford Review, September 22, 1938.

Bryan, Lt. Cmdr. J., III, *Aircraft Carrier*. New York, 1968.

Casey, Louis S., *The First Nonstop Coast to Coast Flight and the Historic T-2 Airplane*, Washington, D.C., 1964.

Dietrich, Noah, and Bob Thomas, *Howard: The Amazing Mr. Hughes*. New York, 1972.

Duke, Neville, and Edward Lanchbery, eds., *The Saga of Flight*, New York, 1961.

Emme, Eugene, ed., *Two Hundred Years of Flight in America*. San Diego, Calif., 1977.

Ethell, Jeff, *Cowboys and Indians*. Alexandria, Va., 1977.

Funderburk, Thomas R., *The Fighters, Men and Machines of the First Air War*. New York, 1965.

Gann, Ernest K., *Ernest K. Gann's Flying Circus*. New York, 1974.

Gibbs-Smith, Charles H., *The Aeroplane*. London, 1960.

———, *Aviation*. London, 1970.

Gill, Brendan, *Lindbergh Alone*. New York, 1977.

Gordon, Arthur, and the eds. of American Heritage, *The American Heritage History of Flight*. New York, 1962.

Grun, Bernard, *The Timetables of History*. New York, 1975.

Hall, James Norman, and Charles Nordhoff, *Falcons of France*. New York, 1929.

Hallion, Richard P., *American Flight Research and Flight Testing: An Overview from the Wright Brothers to the Space Shuttle*. Society of Experimental Test Pilots, vol. 13, No. 3.

———, *Legacy of Flight: The Guggenheim Contribution to American Aviation*. Seattle, 1977.

———, ed., *The Wright Brothers: Heirs of Prometheus*. Washington, D.C., 1978.

Jeffries, John, *A Narrative of the Two Aerial Voyages*. London, 1786.

Jobe, Joseph, *The Romance of Ballooning*. New York, 1971.

Johnson, Group Capt. J.E., *Wing Leader*. New York, 1969.

Kelly, Fred C., *The Wright Brothers*. New York, 1966.

———, ed., *Miracle at Kitty Hawk: The Letters of Wilbur and Orville Wright*. New York, 1951.

Lehman, Milton, *This High Man*. New York, 1963.

Letters from France of Victor Chapman. New York, 1919.

Lindbergh, Charles A., *The Spirit of St. Louis*. New York, 1952.

McFarland, Marvin W., ed., *The Papers of Wilbur and Orville Wright*. 2 vols. New York, 1953.

Mason, Herber Molloy, Jr., *The Lafayette Escadrille*, New York, 1964.

Mikesh, Robert C., *Excalibur III, The Story of a P-51 Mustang*. Washington, D.C., 1978.

———, *Japan's World War II Balloon Bomb Attacks on North America*. Washington, D.C., 1973.

Mohler, Stanley R., and Bobby H. Johnson, *Wiley Post, His Winnie Mae, and the World's First Pressure Suit*. Washington, D.C., 1971.

Mosely, Leonard, *Lindbergh, A Biography*. New York, 1976.

Oakes, Claudia M., *United States Women in Aviation Through WW I*. Washington, D.C., 1978.

Reynolds, Quentin, *They Fought for the Sky*. New York, 1957.

Robinson, Douglas H., *Giants in the Sky, A History of the Rigid Airship*. Seattle, 1973.

Sakai, Saburo, with Martin Caidin, *Samurai!* New York, 1978.

Spenser, Jay P., *Aeronca C-2, The Story of the Flying Bathtub*. Washington, D.C., 1978.

———, "Flak Bait," *Airpower Magazine*, vol. 8., no. 5, Sept., 1978.

Taylor, C. Fayette, *Aircraft Propulsion*. Washington, D.C., 1971.

Index

Numbers in roman type refer to text pages. Numbers in *italic* type refer to pages on which illustrations appear.